Ministry for the Third Millennium

21 BRIDGES TO THE 21ST CENTURY

LYLE E. SCHALLER

ABINGDON PRESS / Nashville

21 BRIDGES TO THE 21ST CENTURY

Copyright © 1994 by Abingdon Press

This book is printed on recycled, acid-free paper.

SCHALLER, LYLE E.
    21 bridges to the 21st century / Lyle E. Schaller.
    p.   cm. — (Ministry for the third millennium)
    ISBN 0-687-42664-2 (pbk. : alk. paper)
    1. Pastoral theology.   2. Twenty-first century—Forecasts.
I. Title.   II. Title: Twenty one bridges to the 21st century.
III. Series.
BV4011.S328   1994
253'.0112—dc20   93-8278
                                                  CIP

93 94 95 96 97 98 99 00 01 02—10 9 8 7 6 5 4 3 2 1

MANUFACTURED IN THE UNITED STATES OF AMERICA

21 BRIDGES TO THE 21ST CENTURY

To
Les Hoffmann,
friend, colleague, fellow explorer,
pastor, entrepreneur, guide,
and missionary

CONTENTS

Contents

INTRODUCTION

Why read a new book on the pastoral ministry in the twenty-first century?[1] After all, will there be that much discontinuity between doing ministry in 1994 and 2004 to justify reading another book? With the exception of the arrival of the gasoline powered automobile and electric lights, there was not a great change between 1885 and 1915 in how to do ministry, was there? The answer to that question is in the difference between the word *change* and the word *changes*. The degree of change between 1885 and 1915 was relatively modest. Urbanism and unprecedented waves of immigration from Europe were the two big changes, but the effects of both were incremental, not sudden.

The past five decades have brought a huge array of changes that have transformed life in America and radically altered the role of the churches. That point can be illustrated by looking quickly at four dozen changes that have occurred during the lifetime of most readers of this book. This list probably will evoke at least five sets of reactions among the readers.

1. Boredom among those who prefer interpretation, commentary, and predictions to statistics. These readers may prefer to skip this section and move on to the first chapter.
2. Dismay at the omission of what those readers identify as the most significant event of the past half century, such as the war in

Vietnam, the fall of the Berlin Wall, the negotiations to create a European Economic Community, the dissolution of the Union of Soviet Socialist Republics, the birth of their first child, the closing of their favorite restaurant, the election of a Democratic president in November 1992, the widespread legalization of gambling by all but two states during the 1980s and early 1990s, the sensitivity to the issue of sexual harassment, the emergence of Japan as a world power, or the publication of their own book.

3. Frustration with the absence of detailed commentary about the implications of these trends.

4. Overdue sleep.

5. Gratitude for a useful sermon illustration.

Another group will be pleased to learn that the implications of a few of these forty-eight changes will be discussed in greater detail in a subsequent chapter.

Two reasons are offered for beginning with these four dozen changes. The first is to reinforce the point that the third millennium will bring a radically different context for ministry than the context of 1901 or 1951 or even 1981. The second reason is to illustrate the impossibility of identifying and discussing all of the changes affecting the pastoral ministry in the early years of the twenty-first century. What are these four dozen changes?

1. For every retired minister in 1950, there were five others serving as parish pastors. By 1992 that ratio had changed to one retiree for every three pastors in congregations (including associates and assistants). In at least four denominations, that ratio is now one retired minister for every two fully credentialed parish pastors. This change has significant financial implications for denominational budgets for pensions and health insurance. (This also is a price the denomination must pay for encouraging pastors to abstain from the use of alcohol and tobacco.)

2. The shift from a multi-story society to a one-story culture has made obsolete tens of thousands of church basements and second-floor sanctuaries.

3. The radical changes in the dress code for teachers, preachers, office workers, senior citizens, and students has changed the appearance of the typical congregation on Sunday morning.

4. Several of the governmental goals concerning education, housing, health care, and family income of the mid-twentieth century were transformed into entitlements by the beginning of the twenty-first century. This has encouraged the concept of entitlements in denominational goal setting.

5. The numerical decline of several mainline denominations has been more than offset by the numerical growth of new Protestant denominations and the emergence of thousands of new independent congregations. This has radically changed the face of American Protestantism in both urban and suburban America and has shattered conventional stereotypes about American Protestantism.[2]

6. The Consumer Price Index quadrupled from 31 in 1964 to 124 in 1989 and stood at 145 in mid-1993. This longest and greatest inflationary wave in American history has had an impact on church finances in general and the staffing of smaller congregations in particular.

7. The number of farms of 50 acres or more in size shrank from 4.2 million in 1935 to slightly over 1.1 million in 1992, but the number of small farms with annual sales of less than $10,000 has grown to over one million, reflecting that increase in urban workers who want to combine a city paycheck with country living. This has reshaped the future constituency for thousands of rural congregations.

8. The founding of the Universal Fellowship of Metropolitan Community Churches in 1968 and its emergence as one of the fastest growing denominations in American Protestantism reflects a change in views of human sexuality and the inability of most churches to be truly inclusive.

9. The number of adults eating breakfast out of the home is now in the millions, and one-fourth eat breakfast on the way to work. One result is that a growing number of churches now begin the Sunday morning schedule with breakfast.

10. The growing affluence of the American people is reflected in the two- or three-car garage with a wide paved driveway that has replaced the two tracks in the grass and the carport. One result is that two or three vehicles are now required to bring the same number of people to church that came in one car in 1955.

11. Immediate satisfactions have replaced deferred gratification as a central component of the American life-style and has changed the way churches design their ministries with youth.

12. The contemporary religious revival has been accompanied by the arrival of a new approach to proclaiming the Gospel through music with the result that music has replaced doctrine as the most divisive issue in thousands of congregations.

13. For literally tens of thousands of children the church has replaced the home and the public school as the primary channel for transmitting traditional moral values and traditional standards for ethical behavior from one generation to the next.

14. The number of milk cows in the United States dropped from 22.2 million in 1930 to 10.1 million in 1990, but in 1990 the average dairy cow in the United States produced 14,645 pounds of milk, more than triple the average of 4,508 pounds in 1930. The result was fewer than one-half as many cows produced nearly one and one-half times as much milk. One result has been the closing of hundreds of farming community churches.

15. Competence, Christian commitment, character, and performance have moved ahead of age, tenure, educational credentials, blood lines, and social status as the decisive criteria in choosing new congregational leaders, both lay and clergy. One result is a huge number of disappointed seekers of power and prestige who believe that the old criteria should still control the selection process.

16. The increase in the total compensation for a fully credentialed and full-time pastor has priced thousands of smaller congregations out of the ministerial marketplace and reduced the proportion of churches with two or three or four clergy on the staff.

17. The proportion of American men, age 60 to 64 years, who were in the labor force dropped from 83 percent in 1950 to 55 percent in 1992, while the proportion of women in that same age bracket who were in the labor force rose from 24 percent in 1950 to 36 percent in 1992, thus radically altering the sources of volunteers for churches and other voluntary associations.

18. The number of registered passenger cars per 1,000 population in the United States jumped from 265 in 1950 to 494 in 1975 to 612 in 1993. One result is the almost total disappearance of the geographical parish.

19. In 1991, Chrysler Corporation spent an amount equal to $1,100 per vehicle on health-care costs, while in thousands of churches the cost of the pastor's health insurance now exceeds the amount of money in that church's budget for missions and benevolences, thus changing the financing of missionary ventures.

20. The proportion of Christian congregations in the United States that have been in existence for at least forty years in 1990 was more than double the proportion in 1950. This has sparked interest in ways to renew or revitalize or redevelop long-established churches.

21. In October 1992, for the first time in American history, the number of government jobs—18,410,000—exceeded the number of manufacturing jobs—18,388,000, according to the United States Bureau of Labor Statistics. This has caused people to ask whether managerial procedures in the churches and denominational agencies are now reflective of governmental procedures.

22. The number of arrests for driving under the influence (DUI) more than doubled from 73 per 10,000 licensed drivers in 1976 to 179 per 10,000 licensed drivers in 1985. This supports the argument that immediate personal satisfactions gradually have eroded neighbor-centered concerns.

23. The number of Americans living on farms dropped from 30.5 million in 1940 to 4.6 million in 1990—a trend that raises

serious questions for the thousands of farming community churches founded between 1800 and 1920.

24. In 1988, 19.3 percent of American-born residents of the United States, age twenty and over, had completed four or more years of college, compared to 57.5 percent for residents of the United States also age twenty and over born in India, 48.7 percent for U.S. residents born in the Philippine Islands, 42.8 for those born in China, 41 percent for those born in Korea, 30.5 percent for those born in Japan, 18.9 percent for those born in Vietnam, and 2 percent for those born in Mexico—these differences raise interesting questions for the policy makers on evangelism in those denominations that draw largely from well-educated churchgoers and that seek to reach recent immigrants.

25. Enrollment in Roman Catholic elementary schools dropped from 4.4 million in 1960 to 1.9 million in 1992, while enrollment in Protestant elementary schools tripled between 1960 and 1990 and now exceeds the enrollment in Catholic schools—the Christian day school has become the most effective single channel for predominantly Anglo congregations to reach (a) black families and (b) upwardly mobile parents regardless of race who place a premium on the values of formal education.

26. Among American families with (a) a family income of $50,000 or over in 1985 and (b) children in grades 1-12, 20.2 percent of the Hispanic children and youth were enrolled in church-related schools, as were 15.1 percent of the white children and 9.3 of the black children. Should Protestant congregations view Christian day schools as a vehicle for reaching ethnic minority parents?

27. The number of Americans age 65 and over doubled from 16.5 million in 1960 to 33 million in 1992. This is a powerful sign of hope for those denominations specializing in reaching mature adults.

28. In 1952 voters with an eighth-grade education or less outnumbered voters who had attended college by a 3-1 margin. In 1992 voters who had attended college outnumbered those who

had an eighth-grade education or less by a 3½ to 1 ratio. This has obvious implications for the teaching ministries and for preaching.

29. One thousand dollars invested at 6 percent interest in 1917, with all interest income reinvested at 6 percent, would have grown to approximately $80,000 by 1992. One thousand dollars invested in the General Electric Company in 1917, exclusive of cash dividends, would have been worth slightly over $280,000 in 1992, while $1,000 invested in Sears Roebuck in 1917 would have been worth $86,000 in 1992, and $1,000 invested in U. S. Steel in 1917 would have been worth $3,800 in 1992, all exclusive of cash dividends. Those investments raise interesting questions about the investment of pension and endowment funds.

30. The best high school athletes can jump farther and sprint faster than Jesse Owens did in the 1936 Olympics, but are the high school students of today more skilled in mathematical and communication skills than their counterparts of 1936? This raises interesting questions about what public high schools do best.

31. The proportion of deaths in the United States that were followed by the cremation of the body doubled from 9 percent in 1979 to 19 percent in 1992. This reflects a change in the traditional American view of death and what happens at memorial services.

32. In 1970 only one-half of all American women aged 25-44 were employed outside the home. By 1990 that proportion had jumped to 75 percent. Who attends the day circles in the women's organization?

33. In 1992, 46 percent of domestic spending by the United States government was allocated to the elderly and 10 percent to children. This reflects the fact that mature adults are far more likely to vote in Congressional and presidential elections than are four year olds and seven year olds. A parallel trend is that in many churches the Sunday morning schedule reflects the preferences of adults rather than the needs of children.

34. For every 1,000 Korean Americans the Bureau of the Census counted 102 Korean-owned businesses. For every 1,000 Americans born in India there were 75 Indian-owned businesses in 1992. For every 1,000 American-born whites there were 67 white-owned businesses. For every 1,000 black Americans there were 14 black-owned businesses. Does this suggest one approach by which the churches will work with all ethnic minority groups?

35. In 1910 there was one Roman Catholic priest in the United States for every 867 Catholics. By 1942 that ratio had changed to one priest for every 617 Catholics, and in 1962 it was one priest for every 771 Catholics. A 1990 study prepared for the National Conference of Catholic Bishops predicted that in 2005 that ratio will be one priest for every 2,200 parishioners. The number of men enrolled in Roman Catholic seminaries dropped from 10.6 per 10,000 Catholics in 1965 to 1.1 per 10,000 Catholics in 1990. The number of women entering a Roman Catholic religious community dropped from 4,110 in 1965 to 506 in 1971.

36. The number of overseas telephone calls made by Americans rose from 23.4 million in 1970 to 199.6 million in 1980 to over one billion in 1990. The number of calls to a toll-free 800 number has increased from 7 million in 1967 to 1.4 billion in 1980 to nearly 11 billion in 1992. Is the telephone replacing letter writing for pastors?

37. According to statistics produced by Veronis, Suhler & Associates, the average adult American spends approximately nine hours daily receiving messages from the media, including radio, television, motion pictures, newspapers, recorded music, videotapes, magazines, and billboards. The competition in communicating the message of Jesus Christ is far greater than it was in 1955.

38. The arrest rate for juveniles, ages 10-17, charged with a violent crime tripled in twenty-five years from 145 per 100,000 in 1965 to 440 per 100,000 in 1990. Should the churches spend more money on security programs or on ministries with families that include children?

39. Of all Jews who married before 1965 and who were still alive in 1992, 89 percent married another Jew and 2 percent married someone who converted to Judaism. Of all persons who were Jewish by birth and who married in the 1985–91 period, only 43 percent married another Jew and 5 percent married someone who converted to Judaism. The number of Protestant-Catholic marriages quadrupled between 1950 and 1990. What is the role of Protestant churches in interfaith marriages?

40. In 1985 private schools accounted for 14.2 percent of the total enrollment grades 1-12 in the Northeast, 12.4 percent in the North Central states, and 8.2 percent in both the South and the West. Will that pattern of private schools continue to spread from the Northeast to the South and the West?

41. Approximately 88 percent of all women born during the 1930s gave birth to at least one child before their thirtieth birthday, compared to 66 percent of the women born in the 1908–12 era and 70 percent of the women born in the 1950s. Likewise, 92 percent of the women born in the 1930s who survived to their fiftieth birthday became mothers, compared to only 65 percent of the women born in 1910 and an estimated 85 percent of those born in 1950. What does this suggest for program planning by leaders in your women's organization?

42. In 1977 a Roper survey revealed that 60 percent of the American population identified themselves as middle class and 22 percent called themselves lower-middle or lower class. A parallel survey in 1992 found only 51 percent identified themselves as middle class and 32 percent declared they were lower-middle or lower class. What does this say to self-identified middle class churches and denominations?

43. The Council on Environmental Quality reported in 1991 that lead pollution in the air in the United States dropped by 93 percent between 1975 and 1989, sulfur dioxide was down 46 percent, carbon monoxide decreased by 47 percent, particulate matter dropped 20 percent, nitrogen oxide decreased 17 percent, and ozone was down 14 percent since 1975. Is this at least in part a result of the teaching of stewardship by the churches?

44. In 1965 approximately 45 million people went to the movies every week. In 1992 that figure was down to 19 million despite a 30 percent increase in the American population. Has the arrival of the "couch potato" and the VCR also undermined the Sunday evening church service?

45. Infant mortality in the United States has dropped from 100 deaths during the first year of life for every 100,000 live births in 1915 to 60 in 1934 to 26 in 1956 to 8.9 in 1991. The life expectancy of the average 40-year-old male in 1955 was 31.7 more years and for the average 40-year-old female in 1955 it was 36.7 additional years. By 1990 those expectations had climbed to 35 more years for 40-year-old men and 41 additional years for women. What is being done to improve the life expectancy of (a) new missions, many of which close before their tenth birthday, and (b) aging congregations?

46. According to Andrew M. Greeley, the proportion of Roman Catholics who believed that premarital sex is always wrong dropped from 74 percent in 1962 to 18 percent in 1992. For non-Catholics that proportion declined from 63 percent in 1962 to 27 percent in 1992.

47. Instead of flaunting a denominational label, a growing number of large congregations are omitting any reference to a denominational identity in choosing a name. (Examples include Cathedral of Hope, Grace Church, House of Prayer, Community Church of Joy, Calvary Temple, Christ Church, Perimeter Church, and Saddleback Valley Community Church.) Does this suggest that a denominational identity is perceived as a handicap rather than as an advantage?

48. As recently as January 1991 only 20,000 private electronic bulletin boards were operating out of basements, garages, and spare bedrooms in private homes in the United States that were linked by modems to other computers. By early 1993 that number had at least quadrupled. Will electronic mail be the successor to parish newsletters, pastoral visits, and telephone calls as the next link between parish and parishioner?

A few of these four dozen changes obviously have more immediate implications for the churches than do most of the others, but many other significant trends are missing from the list.

From this observer's perspective, the most significant single change is the theme of the first chapter. For many decades the two big lines of demarcation that were used to identify the churches in American Protestantism were (a) denominational affiliation and (b) the nationality, racial, or language characteristics of the members. The Welsh Presbyterian, the Swedish Lutheran, the Italian Methodist, and the black Baptist congregations each carried a clear identity that distinguished it from other Presbyterian, Lutheran, Methodist, or Baptist churches.

The 1920s brought a classification system based on where a congregation was located on a theological spectrum. Fundamentalist, liberal, and other terms were used to distinguish one congregation from another within the same tradition.

In the years following World War II, rural, suburban, and urban became useful systems for classifying churches.

Today an argument can be made that denominational labels mean little and the most significant distinction is between those congregations that function as voluntary associations and those that call for a high level of Christian commitment. That is the theme of the first chapter, and it resurfaces in chapters 5, 6, 7, 9, 10, and 12.

A second general theme is that congregational life has been changing dramatically in recent years. That theme appears in chapters 2, 3, 4, 5, 6, 7, 8, 9, 10, 11, 15, and 16 and is especially prominent in chapters 2, 3, 9, 10, and 11.

A third theme is the changing role of denominational agencies, including theological seminaries. That theme appears most clearly in chapters 12, 13, 14, and 16.

A fourth recurring theme is that every congregation, and every denomination, represents a passing parade of people. Every year people leave every parade. Many switch to another parade, a few die, and others simply drop out because they no longer are interested in walking in an ecclesiastical parade. New generations and new immigrants come along. (Perhaps the most relevant statistic for the churches in Los Angeles is that of the 17 million people who migrated from one nation to another during the 1980s, slightly over 5 percent moved to Los Angeles County while another 45 percent moved to other parts of the United States, and one-half moved to some other country on this planet.)

Which will be the numerically growing congregations and denominations in the early decades of the twenty-first century? The answer is those congregations and denominations that are able to attract new generations of American-born adults and new generations of immigrants to their parade.[3] What attracted the generations born before 1945 may not attract many from the new generations. That is the theme of chapters 9 and 16, but it also appears in chapters 2, 3, 4, 6, 7, 8, 10, 12, 13, and 14.

In other words, change is the dominant theme of this book. The response of church leaders to the changes identified here will shape the future of their institutions. More important, however, these responses will determine who will be most effective in proclaiming the gospel of Jesus Christ in the early decades of the third millennium.

1.

THE CALL TO HIGH COMMITMENT

Several years ago an elementary school in the Watts neighborhood of Los Angeles was ranked in the bottom 20 in student achievement among the 650 schools in the entire educational system of that city. That school was filled with underachievers. Conventional wisdom of the day declared the appropriate pedagogical approach with underachievers was to "teach down" to them and emphasize remedial drills and worksheets. The result was a school with a disproportionately large number of children who were labeled "low-achievers" and "at risk."

In 1990 that school adopted a concept pioneered by Stanford University Professor Henry Levin. Levin is convinced that all children can learn and can enjoy learning. He contends that the pedagogical methods traditionally utilized with the most gifted children also can arouse the interest of those identified as "underachievers." If sixth graders are performing at fourth grade level, do not reinforce that by using a fourth-grade curriculum. Challenge the students with tenth-grade material!

By the fall of 1992 more than 300 schools had adopted Professor Levin's concept. Levin estimates six years are required before all the benefits of this approach will be realized.[1] This approach is consistent with a huge body of research that suggests the five crucial components of an effective educational program for children are (1) high expectations, (2) a principal who is committed to excellence, (3) a vigorous curriculum, (4) continuing parental involvement, and (5) homework—which really is one facet of the high expectations and of parental involvement.

What are the distinguishing characteristics of the American Protestant congregations that have been most effective in reaching the generations born after 1945?

Denominational affiliation or theological stance or real estate or location do not make the list. The four characteristics that are most likely to be shared by the congregations reaching large numbers of those generations are (1) the pastor has a strong commitment to excellence; (2) the focus in ministry is not on the institutional agenda of the congregation or denomination, but rather on meaningful responses to the contemporary religious needs of people born after 1945; (3) the leaders project high expectations of people; and (4) membership is not viewed as a destination, but rather as a pilgrimage that leads one toward unreserved discipleship and a higher level of religious commitment (see chap. 10).

One of the most revealing studies on the importance of religious commitment was commissioned by the Connecticut Mutual Life Insurance Company and conducted by Research and Forecasts, Inc., in 1980. The goal was "to probe for the basic beliefs and core values of a diverse cross sampling of Americans."[2]

This study sought to identify the factors that explain a person's values and behavior. Age, for example, often was an especially useful predictor of how a respondent would answer the 175 specific questions asked about values and behavior. Other factors—such as level of educational attainment, income, race, place of residence, occupational status, political orientation, gender, and political party affiliation—also were tested to measure their impact on values and behavior.

To the surprise of the researchers, since this was *not* the purpose of the study, the one variable that stood out above all others as the most reliable predictor for most of the questions was the level of religious commitment. For example, one question asked, "If you had the opportunity, would you like to move somewhere else, or would you stay where you are?" The level of religious commitment followed by age were the two best predictors of how an adult would respond to that question. Gender and income were the least useful predictors. Another question was, "Do you feel you can have a significant influence on the way your community is run?" Those with a high level of religious commitment and blacks were the respondents more likely to reply yes to that question, and those with the lowest level of religious commitment were the most likely to reply no.

In more recent years, various other studies have reported that the level of one's religious commitment also correlates with divorce rates, arrests, probability of graduating from high school, drug use, and even life expectancy.

The Natural Institutional Drift

A review of the history of Protestantism in the Western world indicates that most new religious bodies originally were organized around a call to a high level of religious commitment. That generalization applies to both new denominations and to many new congregations. As the decades roll past, the natural institutional tendency is to drift away from that call to high commitment. Gradually the focus shifts from Christian commitment to "taking care of the members." Kinship and friendship ties, local traditions, institutional survival goals, real estate concerns, and seniority replace Christian commitment as the guiding force in making decisions. In at least a few traditions, a denominational agenda replaces that call to high commitment as the central organizing principle. Most of the numerically growing congregations seek a high level of religious commitment from their members while the low-commitment congregations tend to experience difficulty in reaching new generations of American-born adults and new immigrants to these shores.[3]

Denominational mergers often nudge the commitment level of that tradition toward the low end of the spectrum. This is most evident when a mid-level commitment denomination merges with a religious body closer to the high commitment end of the spectrum. A long series of short pastorates can be an effective means of seriously eroding the religious commitment level of what earlier had been created as a high commitment new mission.

An End-of-the-Century Perspective

A review of North American Protestantism from the end of the twentieth century reveals that (1) the number of congregations that have been in existence for at least five decades stands at an all-time high; (2) the number of low-commitment congregations also is at an all-time high; (3) following the arrival of a new pastor, hundreds of what had become low-commitment churches are now reversing that drift and moving back toward the high commitment end of that spectrum; (4) the most reliable single predictor to distinguish between those congregations (and denominations) that are growing older and smaller and those that are growing younger and larger in numbers is the level of religious commitment; and (5) nearly every effort to revitalize congregations or reform denominational structures is organized around a call to a higher level of Christian commitment.[4]

What Are the Implications?

The numerically growing congregations and denominations of the twenty-first century will not be those that excel in reaching people born before 1940. The numerically growing religious bodies will be those that are organized around excellence, high expectations, facilitating the pilgrimage of their members from a point of low religious commitment to a high level of Christian commitment, and a vision that challenges people to exceed their own self-imposed limitations.

From a congregational perspective, it is clear that a disproportionately large number of today's high-commitment churches were organized since 1960. This simply reflects the fact that it is easier to organize a new mission around the call to a high level of Christian commitment than it is to reverse that drift toward low commitment in a congregation founded fifty or a hundred or more years earlier. A comparison of Protestant churches in New England with those in California illustrates this point. This pattern also illustrates the fact that impatient agents of planned change often choose to create the new rather than seek to reform the old.[5]

As was pointed out earlier, the central component in building a high-commitment congregation is the pastoral leadership. That alone, however, is not sufficient. The magic formula also includes at least two or three volunteers who share that call to high commitment, strong biblical preaching that challenges the listeners to Christian commitment,* and the combination of a challenging teaching ministry and opportunities for being engaged in doing ministry that encourages and facilitates the journey toward full discipleship.

That definition of parish ministry can be seen in both the new missions organized around high commitment and in aging congregations that have reversed that drift and are moving back toward high commitment. That definition of parish ministry will become more widely followed in the twenty-first century. One expression of that approach to high commitment is to make membership more meaningful (see chap. 10).

What Is the Denominational Role?

Eight of the most influential contributions a denomination can make to increasing the number of its high-commitment churches are to: (1) increase the supply of highly skilled, creative, productive, deeply committed, and visionary pastors who believe in this concept of building high-commitment congrega-

---

*A growing pattern requires two different worship experiences on Sunday morning. In one the sermon is designed to speak to the agenda of the pilgrims, inquirers, seekers, and searchers. In the other, the sermon is designed to challenge believers to a deeper level of Christian commitment.

tions; (2) encourage the matching of these pastors in the ministerial placement process with those congregations that have the potential to become high-commitment churches; (3) organize most, if not all, new missions as high-commitment congregations; (4) encourage long pastorates of fifteen to forty years; (5) create the resources to be used by congregational leaders in discipling programs; (6) offer a broad range of challenging opportunities for volunteers to be engaged in doing ministry outside that parish as part of that discipling process; (7) help congregational leaders develop meaningful responses to the religious needs of new generations of people on a religious pilgrimage; and (8) encourage congregational leaders to see the act of uniting with a congregation as one stage in a religious pilgrimage, not as a destination.

Denominations can undermine the call for more high-commitment congregations by (1) encouraging short pastorates of five to ten years; (2) encouraging or requiring congregations to place denominational goals at the top of the agenda of parish priorities; (3) placing credentials above commitment, competence, and character in screening candidates for ordination (see chap. 12); (4) affirming the primary role of congregations to serve as adult employment centers for seminary graduates in need of jobs; (5) encouraging congregational mergers; (6) cutting back on the number of new high-commitment missions launched each year in order to resource (and thus reward) congregations organized around institutional survival goals; and (7) "promoting" exceptionally effective pastors of high-commitment congregations into denominational staff positions.

These last two paragraphs also can be used as diagnostic checklists to identify which denominations will be most effective in reaching the new generations of churchgoers of the twenty-first century.

2.

RULES TO RELATIONSHIPS

In a landmark book published back in 1972, William Glasser offered a three-point diagnosis of contemporary reality. Glasser wrote that he "found that people needed involvement as a prerequisite to change . . . involvement [is] also a prerequisite to a successful role or identity." "The change from a survival or goal society to a successful role society is here." "The institutions of our society still operate as if goal took precedence over role."[1]

Glasser's thesis illustrates one of the most far reaching changes of the second half of the twentieth century. The traditional emphasis in American culture on rules gradually has been eroded. The replacement has been a greater value placed on relationships. This trend can be seen in the evolution of the role of parents in rearing children; in the replacement of the old rule book for teenagers by the peer dimension of the contemporary youth culture on the high school campus; by the changing role of wives in both the home and the labor force; by the increased emphasis on the relational dimensions of life in preaching, evangelism, and teaching; in the expectations projected by today's teenagers toward adults responsible for working with youth; in the administration of hospitals and nursing homes; in the role of a supervisor or "boss" in the business world; in the policing of neighborhoods in large cities; in the speeches of candidates for public office; in the training of teachers; in the public image banks seek to project to their customers; in the growing tendency by candidates for public office to encourage the use of nicknames ("Jimmy" and "Bill" are two recent examples); and in the use of first names by husbands and wives in addressing their mother-in-law or father-in-law. In these and many other dimensions of life, relationships have moved ahead of the traditional rules on the list of priorities.

Not everyone is happy with this trend. Many mothers still prefer to hear that their daughter is planning to follow the traditional rule book about planning a wedding rather than entering "into a relationship" with some young man. Other parents wish that there was a greater emphasis on rules and less on relationships when their daughter leaves home to live in a co-ed dormitory on the university campus. Many divorced mothers would prefer to see that ex-husband first live up to the child support rule in the divorce agreement rather than concentrate only on visitation privileges. A substantial number of the older members still prefer to address the new minister as "Pastor" or "Reverend" or "Doctor" rather than to accept the invitation to "call me by my first name."

Perhaps the biggest contrast in this trend is between the actions of congregations and the legislation adopted by the delegates to the national denominational convention. These national conventions often tend to resemble Old Testament meetings, with the primary focus on the law. The words *shall* and *shall not* are used more than the word *may*. Most legislative proposals are designed as permission-withholding or permission-granting statements. This is most often the pattern when the subject under discussion is money or ordination or abortion or language or sexual orientation or marriage or divorce or the role of women in the church or other issues that lend themselves to inducing guilt.

By contrast, more and more congregations are responding from a New Testament perspective that emphasizes grace and forgiveness when the issue under discussion is the pregnancy of the pastor's unmarried sixteen-year-old daughter or a deacon's gay son who is dying of an AIDS-related illness or the decision of the thirty-nine-year-old mother of five to seek an abortion or the ordination of that exceptionally competent staff member who chose a transdenominational seminary rather than to attend a seminary affiliated with that denomination or the embezzlement of funds by the treasurer who has held that office for three decades or the dissolution of the pastor's marriage or the remarriage of the pastor whose wife died after a long terminal illness only ten months ago.

It is easy for those who are most comfortable in looking for proof texts for their point of view to find verses in the four Gospels that defend permission-withholding. It is even easier to find verses that encourage compassion, love, affirmation, forgiveness, and an acceptance of God's grace.

A second example of the shift from rules to relationships can be seen in the evolution of parish newsletters. Once they were filled with the law about the obligations of members to participate in this, to volunteer for that, to contribute money for this cause, to attend that upcoming meeting, to enjoy reading about the travels or the hobbies of the pastor, or to get behind an organizational goal being promoted by that denomination.

Today the most widely read church newsletters devote most of their space to describing how people's lives have been changed by God's grace, to significant events and happenings in the lives of members, to expressions of gratitude and praise for the work of volunteers, and to promises of what tomorrow will bring.

Perhaps the most significant illustration of this change from rules to relationships can be seen in the content of the pastoral prayer. Once upon a time these prayers were read from a book or carefully written out in advance to be liturgically correct in case a seminary professor happened to be in the congregation that day. Today the pastoral prayer is more likely to lift up the intercessions of the people in that room, to reflect the joys and concerns of this gathered community, and to stress the relationship between God and his people.

Similarly, today's sermons are more likely to focus on God's grace, on the relational dimensions of the faith, on hope, and on Jesus as Lord and Savior rather than on rules that people must obey to prove that they are Christians. To the surprise of those who cling to obsolete stereotypes, this change often is most apparent in theologically conservative and evangelical congregations founded before 1930. Worship today is unlike what it was in 1935 or 1955.

In a growing number of denominations and in many congregations, this shift is reflected in a variety of pronouncements. What once were rigid rules have now become guidelines. What once were demands are now stated as expectations. What once were high pressure campaigns have become low pressure efforts. The big exception to that set of generalizations is those denominations that have evolved from resourcing congregations into regulatory agencies (see chap. 14).

How Do You Draw the Circle?

This change also can be illustrated by looking quickly at a half dozen riddles.

1. What is the difference between the theologically liberal congregation and the fundamentalist church?

The traditional answer, which no longer applies universally to either type, was that the liberal church draws the circle to include people and the fundamentalist congregation draws the circle to exclude.

2. What is the difference between 1953 and 1993 in regard to the frequency of Holy Communion?

In 1953 nearly every Protestant congregation in North America offered one of two pairs of choices. One set of choices declared, "We have Holy Communion every Sunday morning. If you believe that is too frequent, go elsewhere." The other set of choices was, "We have Holy Communion once a quarter (or once a month); if you believe that is too infrequent, you should go elsewhere."

Forty years later, a rapidly growing number of congregations offer this choice, "The early service includes Holy Communion every Sunday, and the second service includes Holy Communion one Sunday every month" (see chap. 9).

3. What is the difference between 1980 and 1990 in regard to smoking on the premises?

In 1980 the most common signs on this subject were NO SMOKING or NO SMOKING! They were designed to make smokers feel completely excluded. In 1990 it was far more common to see signs that read SMOKING IS PERMITTED ONLY IN THE LOBBY or THANK YOU FOR NOT SMOKING or SMOKING PERMITTED ONLY IN DESIGNATED AREAS. These signs were designed to affirm the existence of smokers.

4. What is the difference between new missions and long-established congregations?

New missions usually are designed to make first-time visitors feel welcome and included. Most long-established congregations tend to make first-time visitors feel like intruders or trespassers or excluded.

5. What is the difference between the bank building designed and constructed in 1920 and the one designed and constructed in 1990?

The one designed in 1920 often conveyed the image of a fortress designed to protect the money and repel poor people, strangers, and bank robbers. The bank designed and constructed in 1990 conveys the impression this is a place that welcomes those who never have been here before. A parallel distinction can be drawn between many old and some new church buildings. The most obvious illustration of old and new designs in church buildings is in the width of the corridors. In 1950 corridors were designed to enable people to walk from Point A to Point B. In 1990 the corridors in church buildings were much wider to encourage informal conversations and fellowship, to be utilized as channels of communication, to make strangers feel welcome, to facilitate people-watching, to help convey a distinctive congregational image, and also to serve as pedestrian walkways.

6. *What is the difference between a congregation and a denomination?*

Denominations tend to concentrate on articulating and enforcing permission-withholding rules and on exclusionary criteria, while congregations nurture people on their religious pilgrimage by placing the top priority on strengthening relationships and on inclusion.

One of the purposes of churchwide or denominational conventions is to identify the people we want to keep out (see Acts 15:1-6). The healthy congregation of today stands with Peter and agrees that the focus should be on God's love and inclusion, not on the genitalia of a person. Through the centuries, however, churchwide gatherings have chosen to focus on the genitalia in efforts to build walls of exclusion.

What Are the Implications?

The most obvious implication of this trend is that the churches seeking to reach and serve the generations born since 1942 will be more effective if they build their ministry around the concepts and values reflected in such words as *grace, relationships, hope, love, forgiveness, identity, acceptance, compassion, choices, caring,* and *service.* Those seeking to reach and serve the generations born before 1920 probably will continue to be more comfortable concentrating on rules, the law, permission-withholding, and judgment.

For many executives of regional judicatories, the most painful implication comes with the choosing of sides. In intradenominational disputes, should the executive and staff of that regional judicatory choose to stand with the congregational leaders or seek to affirm and support the legalistic rules of the national denominational agencies? Frequently this comes down to a choice between law and grace.

The most significant implication of this change from rules to relationships already is apparent in the governance of congregations. On the one side are those congregations in which the system of governance is built around permission-withholding. In several traditions this is reinforced by the self-identified role by the denomination as a regulatory agency (see chap. 14). Most changes, the addition of new ministries and programs, new ventures in community outreach, or any expansion of existing ministries must be approved by a majority vote. If more negative votes than affirmative voices are cast, the proposal is dead. In some traditions a new idea may be approved by a majority vote of the members, but vetoed by the regional judicatory or a national agency of that denomination. In literally hundreds of congregations the final outcome was decided by which side was able to motivate most of its supporters to come to that meeting.

In a growing number of congregations, however, the focus is not on counting those no votes. Instead, the emphasis is on counting the yes votes. Do we have the fifteen people we need to justify creating a new adult Sunday school class? If so, we do it. We do not offer those who will never attend that class the opportunity to veto it. Do we have a dozen members who will contribute $5,000 for the partial support of a missionary? If we believe we do, we ask for those contributions. We do not give the ninety members who will not support missions the opportunity to veto that special emphasis. Do we have a dozen volunteers who will staff a second week of vacation Bible school in mid-August? If we do, we schedule that second week.

The crucial distinction is trust. Do we trust the ideas, the intentions, and the integrity of what is clearly a minority? The greater the emphasis on nurturing healthy relationships, the more likely the response will be affirmative. The greater the dependence on rules, the more likely the response will be to look to precedents, tradition, and the rule book for an answer.

Which congregations will be most successful in building new ministries with new generations of people in the twenty-first century? Those that are organized around permission-withholding and exclusionary rules or those that place a premium on nurturing the relational aspects of life that enable the members to trust the leaders and lean in the direction of permission-granting? Which denominational systems will have to be transformed to encourage nurture and inclusion?

Likewise, those institutions that place survival goals at the top of the priority list may encounter frustrating difficulties as they watch where the generations born after 1942 go to church. These younger generations are less likely to be attracted by the importance of survival goals. They are more likely to be found in those congregations that are highly intentional about their identity, role, and ministry.

Finally, being asked to serve as a delegate to the annual meeting of a national denominational gathering or a regional judicatory has been compared to going to the dentist for a root canal procedure. In both experiences, the reward is that eventually it is over.

Which denominational meetings do you believe people will look forward to attending in the twenty-first century? Those organized around adopting legalistic responses to controversial issues, defining the criteria for exclusion, debating new permission-withholding rules, creating new regulations to govern the ministry of congregations and making decisions on means-to-an-end issues with a series of close votes?

Or will volunteers look forward more eagerly to denominational conventions organized around renewing old friendships, joyous singing, inspirational worship, hope, warm fellowship, inclusion, celebrations of victories achieved, proclamation of God's word, affirmation of the ministries of the churches, grace, recognition of the efforts of the saints, challenges for tomorrow, and the adoption of new goals for ministry?

3.

THE MOST STARTLING CHANGE

I n the early 1950s the experts were recommending three
acres for the site of a new congregation. One explanation
was, "You need an acre for parking, an acre for your building, and an acre for setbacks and landscaping." To many
church leaders, this appeared to be an extravagant criterion, so
they established their new mission on a site of an acre or less.

By the late 1960s, most of the experienced specialists in new
church development were recommending five to seven acres as
the minimum size for the site for a future meeting place for a
new congregation.

By the early 1980s, the chickens were coming home to roost.
Scores of congregations organized in the decades following
World War II were discovering that success brought insur-
mountable problems. The limitations of that original site not
only placed a ceiling on future growth, but those limitations
often undercut contemporary programing as well.

The typical initial response to this problem of limited space
was to attempt to make the best of a bad situation. These efforts
included razing the parsonage next door and either replacing it
with an educational wing or paving that area for parking. Other
congregations purchased adjacent property—and still found
themselves short of space. The typical pattern began with the
reluctant recognition that additional land was needed. Someone
proposed that the best long-term solution would be to relocate
and build new. That was rejected by an overwhelming majority.
The next step was to acquire additional land for expansion and

invest more money in capital improvements. After these were completed, a space problem still existed. Finally, after lengthy discussions and endless meetings, the decision was made to relocate. The first recommendation was to purchase a seven- to fifteen-acre site a few miles away. Sometimes this became the new course of action. In other situations, that recommendation was rejected in favor of purchasing a much larger and more distant site at a better location.

One congregation chose to sell the nine-acre original site and purchase a fifty-acre parcel. Another left a seven-acre location for a fifteen-acre new location. A third sold the original thirty-five-acre site as part of the plan to relocate to a 105-acre parcel. A fourth is relocating from a nineteen-acre site to a 200-acre parcel. A congregation founded in 1977 is relocating because it has outgrown that original twenty-acre site.

What Happened?

The most highly visible explanation for this need for more land for churches can be illustrated by two sets of statistics. First, in 1940 208 passenger cars were registered in the United States for every 1,000 residents. Ten years later, that ratio had climbed to 265 per 1,000 residents. By 1993 it was up to 612 for every 1,000 residents, three times the 1940 ratio, and the number of licensed motor vehicles exceeded the number of licensed drivers. Second, in 1971, 39 percent of all new single-family homes were constructed with a two-car garage. By 1991 that proportion had climbed to 71 percent.

Two or three times as many vehicles are required to bring one hundred people to church today as were needed in 1955.

A second part of the explanation is that like people, universities, hospitals, grocery stores, and amusement parks, churches are getting larger. The number of Protestant megachurches in America averaging a thousand or more at worship has at least quadrupled since the 1950s. On the average weekend, one-sixth of all Protestant congregations in the United States account for over one-half of the churchgoers. Whether they be discount stores, high schools, or churches, larger institutions require more land.

The most subtle factor in this demand for more land can be described by the single word *scale*. During the first three decades of the twentieth century, it was not uncommon to construct the meeting place for a Protestant congregation that could accommodate (a) 600 at one worship service, (b) 200 in Sunday school, (c) 100 adults seated for a meal at tables in the fellowship hall, (d) one pastor and one church secretary, and (e) zero automobiles in church-owned off-street parking.

Those planning for the twenty-first century assume (a) those pews that allegedly would seat 600 seriously malnourished people back in 1923 are now comfortably filled with 400 of today's healthy adults; (b) the trend toward multiple worship experiences on Sunday morning means that a congregation can average 700 or 800 at worship with a nave that is comfortably filled with 400; (c) the congregation averaging 700 at worship needs to be able to accommodate at least 400 to 600 or more in Sunday school; (d) the space required in 1923 to accommodate 500 in Sunday school now feels crowded with 250 present; (e) the congregation averaging 700 at worship should be able to seat at least one-half that many at tables for a meal in the fellowship hall; (f) with an average worship attendance of 700 at three or four worship experiences every weekend, today's congregation needs office space for at least two ordained ministers, plus three or four other full-time (or equivalent in part-time positions) program staff members plus three or four support staff; (g) at least three acres of land will be paved for off-street parking, and another half acre or more in driveways will be needed for the congregation averaging 700 in worship and 400 to 600 in Sunday school; (h) two or more acres will be needed for outdoor recreational space; (i) the one-story preference of today's adults means that the economical three-story (plus basement) design of 1923 has been replaced with a one-story structure that covers four or five times as much land area; and (j) the local municipal government may require one acre for a storm water detention basin for every acre under roof or paved.

Thus the half-acre site of 1923 has been replaced by the need for at least seven or eight acres to house the same size congregation for the next millennium.

A fourth factor is that today's churchgoers are not as willing to be crowded as were their grandparents. One result is that seven or eight people now fill the pew designed for a dozen. Other consequences include wider corridors, a larger narthex, additional space for new weekday specialized ministries, more spacious meeting rooms, more and larger restrooms, greater setbacks from the street, a much larger chancel, and far more office space.

Likewise, the high-expectation congregation needs more space than the low-expectation congregation. The simplest illustration is that the family of three that comes in two vehicles with one or two of the three being in the building for three or four hours on Sunday morning needs twice the parking and twice the restroom capacity that is required for a family of three who come for one hour on Sunday morning.

Finally, the change in programing and the addition of specialized ministries often means that construction designed for the twenty-first century will include space for a weekday prekindergarten nursery school or perhaps an all-day child-care facility or possibly a K-12 Christian day school, reserved parking near the door leading to the nursery for single parents, a latch-key after-school program, a library, a gymnasium, an adult day-care program, storage for a community food pantry, an outdoor garden columbarium or memorial garden, attractive and comfortable rooms for weekday adult study groups, a bookstore, a counseling center with its own entrance and reception area, space to accommodate a thirty- to forty-person orchestra during worship, the offices for a parachurch organization, outdoor athletic fields, and perhaps a congregationally owned and operated retirement complex or seminary or college or nursing home or wellness center on campus.

The people who found that half-acre site to be completely adequate in 1923 are now in nursing homes and cemeteries. Their grandchildren conclude they need at least ten, and perhaps as many as four hundred, acres for the site of their church.

What Are the Implications?

How much land will a congregation need in the twenty-first century? One factor, of course, is availability and cost. The downtown congregation averaging 700 at worship probably will have to build up, rather than out, and thus may have to "get by" on a relatively small parcel of land. The congregation faced with paying $400,000 an acre for land also is confronted with limitations on what it can do.

For new missions and relocated congregations, however, four guidelines may be of value. First, if possible, acquire twice as much land as your most optimistic and farsighted policy maker believes is necessary. If this respected leader argues for ten acres when most of the other policy makers believe five will be sufficient, purchase twenty acres.

Second, plan to acquire at least three times as much land as contemporary conventional wisdom suggests. Thus the new mission of 1954 that had been advised to purchase three acres—and acquired only one acre—would have been far better off if it had purchased nine acres. Twenty years later, the leaders might have concluded that four acres were sufficient. It would have been much easier in 1974 to find a buyer for those five surplus acres than to find a willing seller for the additional acre or two or three now needed.

Third, what does conventional wisdom suggest as a reasonable size for a church site? At the end of the twentieth century, contemporary conventional wisdom was suggesting a congregation needed one acre of land plus one additional acre for each one hundred people at worship on the typical weekend. Thus the congregation that averaged 200 at the Saturday evening service, 100 at the early Sunday morning service, 300 at the late

Sunday morning worship experience, and 100 on Monday evening was advised it needed a minimum of eight acres.

This may turn out to be an inadequate site in the year 2014 if (a) that congregation continues to grow in size and/or (b) a decision is made to include a Christian day school for children ages three-twelve as part of the total ministry with families that include young children and/or (c) if the neighbors express strong objections to requests for permits for new construction or to an enlargement of the parking area or an expansion of the weekday program (see chap. 15) and/or (d) if that congregation accepts the role of a teaching church[1] and/or if that congregation decides to participate in the movement to shift the training of the next generation of parish pastors from the campus of a theological seminary to the campus of a worshiping community.

For many of us born before or during the Great Depression, the most highly visible and the most startling change is the need for far more land for a church than was thought to be prudent as recently as the 1950s and 1960s. One example of this trend is that big box out on the edge of town.

4.

THE BIG BOXES ARE HERE!

What is one of the biggest concerns of the traditional supermarket that has hit a plateau in the dollar volume of grocery sales? What worries the local pharmacist who owns and operates the drugstore he purchased from his father thirty-five years ago? What is the future of that hardware store that has been in the same family for three generations? What will the future bring to the couple in their fifties who each work sixty hours a week running the small office supply store they opened back in 1970? What is the successor to the "five and dime" variety stores that supplied millions of children in the 1950s with their school supplies, toys, and gifts as well as met many of the shopping needs of their parents?

The answer to all five questions is the same. Each one of these retail outlets has been affected by the arrival of the new large-scale store.[1] The huge "warehouse" grocery stores now sell almost the same dollar volume of groceries as are sold by the conventional supermarkets. The discount drugstores have created stiff competition for the traditional family-owned pharmacies. The mammoth builder's supply stores that stock hardware, paint, and an unbelievable array of building materials draw shoppers from the small hardware store that was a community meeting place on Main Street. The new discount store that sprawls over 80,000 to 140,000 square feet of retail space in front of a couple of acres of parking offers stiff competition to the 6,000 square foot variety store. That big box that has office supplies stacked ten feet above the floor is the new competition for the small office supply store.

The same story can be repeated with the sale of appliances, books, clothing, sewing materials, and toys. The big boxes gradually are replacing the small retailers. These big boxes range in size from 20,000 to 150,000 square feet. They offer a huge range of inventory, low prices, convenient parking near the front door, and limited help for customers with questions. Intimacy has been replaced by anonymity. The relational facets of life have been overshadowed by a new emphasis on efficiency, economy, choice, and privacy.

The scale of what has been happening is illustrated by what used to be called "the dime store." Woolworth, Kresge, and Ben Franklin department stores originally included 3,000 to 6,000 square feet of retail space. The newest KMart stores cover 80,000 to 148,000 feet.

The Ecclesiastical Counterpart

"Reverend, what can you tell me about the new church that meets in the big box of a building out on the west side?" demanded a forty-two-year-old third-generation member of old First Church downtown.

"Not much, I'm afraid," replied the pastor. "All I know is they met in a warehouse out in an industrial park for several years before building that new box, as you call it. Their pastor never comes to our local ministerial association, but I understand they're running close to a thousand on Sunday morning. Their parking lot must hold at least four hundred cars, but I don't know whether they fill it or not. Three or four of our younger families have left here to go out there. My impression, however, is that they reach a different slice of the population than we do. Why do you ask?"

"The reason I ask is that our sixteen-year-old son has been going out there with some of his friends for the past few months," replied this father. "He sort of dropped out of church here after he was confirmed two years ago. He claimed that church bored him. Now he is out there two nights a week plus all Sunday morning. Tuesday evening he is part of a Christian rock music group that he says attracts a couple of hundred teenagers when it performs. Wednesday night he goes to a two-hour Bible study, but he usually is gone for three hours. Sundays he's out there for three or four hours. We always wanted him to be religious, but this seems to be a bit too much. Now he wants my wife and me to come to church there next Sunday, and I wanted to get some idea of what we would be getting into if we went."

"I'm sorry, but I'm afraid I've told you all I know," replied the pastor. "My hunch is that if you do go, you'll find the music is quite a bit different from what we have here at First Church. As you may know, we also have two other new megachurches in town that attract large numbers of people with a similar type of programming—one on the south side, and one that meets in an abandoned movie theater on the east side. But I do not know enough about any of them to give you either a recommendation or a warning."

The big boxes first changed the nature of public education with the consolidation of rural schools. The next wave of big boxes was located out on the edge of town and changed the face of industrial America from three or four stories to one story. A more recent wave is changing the nature of retail trade in America, as was pointed out earlier. Concurrently another wave of big boxes is being constructed to house a rapidly growing number of new congregations.

What Are Your Options?

Have the big boxes housing the new megachurches appeared yet on the ecclesiastical landscapes in your community?

If the answer is no and you are a church in *rural* America, one response is for your church to become what retailers call a "category killer." This is the store that is so dominant it preempts other retailers from competing in that category. Toys "R" Us is a common example. For your rural or small-town congregation, that means redefining your role to that of a regional church, serving people who live within a fifteen- to thirty-mile radius.

How can the typical rural or small-town congregation keep out the competition of a potential new "big box" church?

This probably will require (1) an expansion of the teaching ministry with adults; (2) scheduling two *different* worship experiences on fifty Sunday mornings every year; (3) diversifying the ministry of music; (4) upgrading the quality of all facets of congregational life, including the Sunday school, preaching, off-street parking, restrooms, administration, community outreach, internal communication, meeting rooms, and public relations; (5) developing two or three specialized areas of ministry, such as with young adults or families with teenagers or health or spiritual formation or discipling; and (6) transforming the long-time members' expectations of what tomorrow could bring. For some it also will require relocation to a larger site and a new building.

A second response is to carve out a narrowly and precisely defined niche and be content to be a high-quality small church with a narrow and precisely defined constituency. A third is to reduce expenditures as your numbers shrink and implement a fortress strategy to hang on until no one is left to mourn at the last funeral. A fourth is to merge with another congregation. A fifth is to reduce overhead by becoming part of a cooperative arrangement including two or more congregations. A sixth is to change from a full-time resident pastor to a bivocational pastor or, better yet, a bivocational team. A seventh alternative is to concentrate on a high-quality teaching ministry that includes a Christian day school for children ages three through nine or ten. An eighth is to expand your ministry of music to include at least three music groups in every worship experience.

If you are in a *metropolitan* county, which is where three-quarters of the American population, but less than one-half of all Protestant churches, can be found, one alternative is to join the crowd. Relocate to a forty- or sixty- or hundred-acre site, construct your own big box, concentrate on excellence in ministry, and grow into a megachurch.

A second alternative is to focus on a narrow and precisely defined slice of the theological spectrum. The further to the left that focus is, the more likely you will have to draw a very large circle on the map if you want to average over two hundred at worship.

A third option is to merge. A fourth is to undertake a modest relocation effort to a three- to seven-acre site and start over as a new mission in a new place. A fifth is to meet the payroll by deferred maintenance on the real estate and wait for the arrival of that transformational pastor who will lead you into a new era. A sixth, which is the most demanding, is to transform what is primarily a Sunday morning congregation into a seven-day-a-week program church that includes everything from concerts to athletic teams, to prayer calls, to adult Bible study classes, to after-school programming for elementary-age children, to instruction in music, to quilting clubs, to mutual-support groups, to mission work trips.

A seventh alternative, which can be accomplished with only the enthusiastic and determined leadership of the pastor, is to become a high-commitment congregation that projects high expectations of all members (see chap. 1).

An eighth option is to pretend that this is simply another passing fad and that the big boxes are not here to stay. If we all ignore them, they will go away. That was the choice of hundreds of small-town retailers. That explains why there are so many boarded-up storefronts on Main Street today.

Which is the most attractive option for your congregation as you look forward to more big boxes in the twenty-first century?

5.

PERFORMANCE COUNTS!

Once upon a time American automobile manufacturers had a near monopoly in the marketplace in the United States. During the last third of the twentieth century that changed as German, Japanese, and Korean manufacturers won a larger share of the American market.

Most buyers displayed little interest about the input side of the business. They were not influenced by the size or number of assembly plants, the salary level of the executives, the wages and benefits earned by the workers nor the agreements each corporation had with the suppliers. The primary criteria used by consumers in choosing a new car were quality, price, economy, and reliability. Their evaluations were determined by the output side of the process, not the input.

* * *

One of the goals imposed on the administrators of every theological seminary is to earn accreditation from the regional accrediting associations. This is required for the students to qualify for federal loans. It also may be necessary for foreign students or teachers to secure a visa to visit the United States. Full accreditation also is worth a couple of brownie points in the school's public image.

The usual criteria include such variables as the size of the library, the academic credentials and publications of the faculty, the size of the endowment fund, and the ethnic mix of the student body. On occasion an accrediting team also added the ethnic and/or gender mix of the governing board as a criterion. These are all on the input side of the ledger.

By contrast, more and more congregational and denominational leaders are evaluating theological seminaries by the competence, Christian commitment, and character of the graduates who enter the parish ministry (see chap. 12).

Others are examining the proportion of the graduates who continue to be parish pastors a dozen years after graduation. In one example, 30 percent of the graduating class of 1978 were in the parish ministry a dozen years after graduation. Another nearby seminary in the same denomination reported 80 percent of the 1978 graduates were still parish pastors in 1992. Which of those two schools now receives a substantial financial grant annually from the regional judicatory of that denomination?

Which are the more meaningful indicators in evaluating the performance of a theological seminary? Those on the input side or those on the output side?

* * *

A pastor nominating committee is in the process of interviewing a dozen candidates in the search for a new minister. What should the members of this committee place high on the list of criteria in evaluating these candidates? Age? Academic credentials? Gender? Marital status? Race? Place of birth? Current salary? Physical appearance? Publications? Membership on denominational committees? Travel experiences? Years in the ministry?

Or should the most influential single factor be that candidate's record as a parish pastor? What has happened in the congregation this candidate is now serving?

In several traditions the factors on the input side have been given considerable weight by denominational officials responsible for ministerial placement. Many lay leaders in smaller congregations also tend to be heavily influenced by factors on the input side.

By contrast, lay leaders in (a) large congregations, (b) numerically growing churches, and (c) independent or non-denominational churches tend to be most impressed by a candidate's performance in the parish ministry.

* * *

That rapidly growing number of church shoppers born after World War II may not pay much attention to the denominational label on the building, but they are influenced to at least a modest degree by real estate, newspaper advertisements, television, air conditioning, the degree of emphasis placed on money, and other input considerations.

Far more influential with most of them, however, are two output or performance factors. First, does someone I know and trust unreservedly recommend the ministry of this church to me? Do they assure me that it is meeting their religious needs?

Second, will it offer a meaningful and relevant response to my religious needs?

The generations of Americans born before 1940 were taught to place a high value on factors on the input side. These included (1) the number of dollars spent annually per student by a school, (2) the manufacturer's label on an automobile or article of clothing, (3) years of experience—many salary schedules reward experience rather than performance, (4) the political party affiliation of a candidate for public office, (5) the union label, (6) academic credentials, (7) the quantity and quality of the real estate, (8) the number of paid staff members, (9) the size of the budget, (10) endowment funds, and (11) titles.

The generations born after 1940 place a far lower value on factors on the input side and give much greater weight to performance, quality, and relevance.

As you plan for the future of your congregation or denomination for the twenty-first century, is your top priority reaching people born before 1940 or after 1940?

This distinction between the input and the output or performance can be seen most clearly in several traditions in the criteria for ordination—but that is another chapter.

What Are the Implications?

For congregational leaders, the most significant implication of this contemporary emphasis on performance can be summarized with the same word used by automobile manufacturers: *competition.* The competition among automobile manufacturers today is far more intense than it was in 1948 or 1960.

Likewise, the competition among congregations for the next generation of members is far more intense than it was in the middle of the twentieth century. In 1955, for example, denominational allegiance, kinship ties, inherited institutional loyalties, geographical convenience, and habit were influential factors in picking a church home. Today the capability of a congregation to offer a meaningful response to the religious needs of the church shopper often is the decisive variable in that choice of a church home. This is most highly visible in those congregations seeking to reach and serve adults born after 1955.

The contemporary open recognition that congregations are competing with one another is in marked contrast to the dream of greater intercongregational cooperation of the 1920–1970 era. One of the disillusioning discoveries for me and for many others has been that intercongregational cooperation in programming and numerical growth are mutually incompatible goals.[1]

One product of this new wave of competition among the churches can be summarized by this question from a long-time member. "When we moved here in 1967, this was the largest Protestant church in town. Since then the population of this community has tripled and we now rank seventh in size among the Protestant churches. What happened?"

The answer probably is the performance of that church could not keep up with the competition.

For pastors the most significant implication is, as is discussed in chapter 12, that performance and character have replaced academic credentials as the crucial variables in evaluating candidates for a call.

For denominational leaders, this new emphasis on performance has profound implications. What motivates congregational leaders to send dollars to the denominational headquarters? In 1955 the answer to that question included such factors as institutional loyalty, tradition, a feeling of obligation, a commitment to missions, gratitude, and encouragement from the pastor.

Today a common question is, "What do we get for that money we send to the denominational headquarters? Most of the resources we use are purchased from parachurch agencies. Why should we keep sending money when we don't get anything back for it?"

A second, and more sophisticated, question is, "What are they doing with those dollars? Are they good stewards of what we send them?" This shift from the first to the third person pronoun in referring to the denomination represents an increasing degree of alienation. The best cure for that alienation is proof of high performance.

Finally, back in the 1970s when the church growth movement came to national popularity, much of the discussion was on the input side of the ledger. How do you invite people to your church? Should you add a staff person who will specialize in evangelism? Should the denomination offer financial subsidies to congregations with the potential for substantial numerical growth? Will remodeling that old building attract more new members? What should your evangelism committee do to attract new members?

Today we see scores of large and numerically growing congregations that never invite people to their church. They concentrate all their resources on the performance side of ministry.

Their experience has proved to them that excellence in doing ministry will attract more newcomers than they are able to assimilate. Meaningful worship, transformational preaching, relevant teaching, and a sensitive response to the religious yearnings of people is the best recipe for numerical growth. More important, that also is the best formula for creating high-performance congregations (see chap. 1) that will dominate American Protestantism in the twenty-first century.

6.

CHOICES AND QUALITY

During the last three decades of the twentieth century, the majority of adult Americans have been enjoying a range of choices without parallel in human history. Americans now enjoy an unprecedented degree of freedom on whether or whom to marry and on when to become a parent. Most also are able to choose from a huge array of alternatives in determining their own personal identity, vocation, and place of residence.

Those are five of the most influential experiences in a person's life. For most of human history, those choices were determined largely by birth. Most Americans who reached adulthood before 1930 lived in a culture in which a future spouse would be chosen from a small circle of possibilities. The size and characteristics of the candidates in that circle would be determined largely by parentage and place of birth. Likewise, societal norms influenced the age at which one would marry. Parenthood was largely a product of nature, not of intentionality. The son's occupation usually was determined by the father's occupation.

Marriages were proclaimed to last "until death do us part." The death of a spouse did account for the majority of terminations of existing marriages. In 1959, for example, 395,000 marriages in the United States were terminated by divorce, compared to 526,000 that ended with the death of a spouse. By 1968, however, those proportions had changed dramatically as 584,000 couples saw their marriage end in divorce and 575,000 marriages were terminated by the death of a spouse, usually the husband. With 2,069,000 marriages that year, the result was a net increase of 910,000 in the number of married couples.

The freedom of choice to terminate a marriage continued to spread so that by 1979 58 percent of all marriages in the United States that came to an end in that year were terminated by divorce.

Rather than wait for death to dissolve an unhappy marriage, a majority of unhappy couples are now exercising their choice to turn to the divorce courts. One consequence is that 42 percent of all American women, age sixty-five and older, now live alone.

Today American shoppers can choose from more than 25,000 different items on the shelves of the local supermarket. They can subscribe to one or more of over 11,000 magazines. Many can choose from among nearly five dozen channels on their television set, and that number probably will quadruple before the end of this century. That gourmet store may offer a choice from among sixty-five types of coffee beans and roasting alternatives. The suburban city with 50,000 residents may be the home to two or three dozen churches, a small range of choices compared to the typical rural county with 10,000 residents and thirty to forty churches or that center-city neighborhood with 20,000 residents and sixty churches.

More and more Protestant congregations are not only offering people a choice from among four or five alternatives for the day and time of corporate worship, but also are offering at least three different types of worship experiences every weekend.

Back in the 1950s, many people were confronted with four choices on Christmas Eve. They could (1) worship in their own church, (2) visit and go to church with their parents or their adult children, (3) attend Christmas Eve services with a friend at the friend's church, or (4) not go.

Today it is not uncommon for one congregation to offer five to seven different worship experiences on December 24. The first option is for very young children who may not be able to comprehend the implications of the virgin birth, but do understand the meaning of birthdays, to go to a four o'clock birthday party for Jesus. This service may be followed at five o'clock with one designed with elementary children as the number-one audience. An hour or so later is the "family service" for those who go home to open Christmas presents with the hopes the children will be in bed shortly after eight. These three services are followed, in varying sequences, with Christmas Eve worship experiences built around drama, instrumental music, Holy Communion, a chancel choir, the singing of carols, or preaching.

Once upon a time the adult Sunday school was organized by classifying people by age, gender, and/or marital status. Today the Sunday school may offer a dozen or more adult classes. One is a forum class on applied Christianity. A second is a Bible study with a focus on learning content. A third is on Christian living. A fourth is on doctrine. A fifth is for developmentally disabled adults. A sixth is for young adults. A seventh is for newlyweds in their first marriage. The eighth is the Pilgrim's Class for inquirers, seekers, and searchers on a faith journey. The ninth is for formerly married and now single adults. Another is for empty nesters who enjoy growing old together. Another is a class on parenting skills for those who recently welcomed the arrival of their first child. The twelfth class may be a Bible study taught by the senior minister with over two hundred people of all ages in regular attendance. Another is the Phoenix Class for couples in their second or subsequent marriage. Another is an intergenerational class. A fifteenth is the adult class that creates the study materials used by another class. The sixteenth is for the self-identified charismatic Christians in that congregation. The seventeenth is for couples in an interfaith marriage. The eighteenth is for parents with an adult child dying from AIDS-related causes.

Why?

Why so many choices? One reason is the new generations who have been reared in a culture that teaches people that our society offers many choices and you cannot say yes to all of them. Another reason is that choice is a product of affluence, and ours is an affluent society. A third is that an increasing number of large institutions (universities, supermarkets, shopping malls, apartment buildings, airlines, high schools, churches, medical clinics, etc.) now can mobilize the resources necessary to offer people a remarkable range of choices. A fourth part of the explanation is a word that is heard ever more frequently on the ecclesiastical landscape. That word is *competition*. Many congregational leaders, some reluctantly, feel obligated to expand the range of choices in order to "keep up with the competition." This is most obvious in youth ministries, recreational and sports ministries, trips, adult classes, the Christmas Eve schedule, and music, but that is far from a complete list.

Finally, and perhaps most influential, is the combination of (a) the desire to enhance diversity in the membership and (b) the hope of mixing new generations of churchgoers in with the folks who joined the congregation a couple of decades ago. Expanding that range of choices by creating new choirs, groups, classes, cells, ministries, organizations, and task forces to reach new generations is one means of building an intergenerational fellowship.

The Other Half of the Equation

One of the most common problems created by the desire to expand the range of choices is summarized by this question: "I agree that we need an adult choir for the early service and another adult choir for the late service, but how can we do that without reducing the quality of the music?" That question is based on fixed sum reasoning, which assumes that the number of potential choir members is a fixed figure.

One excessively frequent response is to have a "first class" choir and a "second class" choir that rehearse the same anthem at the same time with the leadership of the same choir director.

The best voices are asked to sing at the second service and the others, plus two or three who will sing at both services, sing at the first hour.

A better response is to seek two different choir directors with two different personalities and two different approaches to music. One rehearses on Thursday evening, and that choir sings at the second service. The other director gathers a different group of people who sing at the first service, attend or teach in the Sunday school in the second period, and rehearse during the last period of the morning.

That approach, however, does not face directly the real issue. The real issue is expectations. Low expectations create a self-fulfilling prophecy. High expectations also can create a self-fulfilling prophecy (see chap. 5).

Today people are not satisfied with the choice between first class and second class or between third rate and fourth rate. They expect *both* choices *and* quality.

For example, a fair number of exceptionally loyal and long-time church members appear willing to settle for a second rate early Sunday morning worship service that does not include an anthem sung by an adult choir. For them, the fact that the early service runs only forty or forty-five minutes is a positive trade-off. Younger churchgoers, however, want *both* choice of time *and* a high quality anthem.

What Are the Implications?

The most obvious implication of this growing demand for more choices is that it should not be met by reducing quality.

The most subtle implication can be summarized by an innocent question, "What do you mean by quality?"

Thousands of small churches can properly brag about their high quality when they point to the quality of the relationships of the pastor and the parishioners, the quality of pastoral care, the quality of the interpersonal relationships among many of the members, and the quality of the individual Christian commitment of the "pillars" in that congregation.

Church shoppers in general, and especially those born after 1955, however, often look first at quality in terms of the parking, the women's restrooms, the nursery, the meeting rooms, the music, the sermon, the teaching, the worship, the ministries with children and youth, the welcome accorded the first-time visitor, and the place of missions and outreach in the local list of priorities.

Quality, like beauty, often is in the eye of the beholder, and it may depend on what that person is viewing. The definition of *quality* may become a divisive issue very easily.

A third implication is for staffing. This combination of choice and quality has produced an escalating demand for both clergy and lay staff who can help a congregation expand choices and raise quality. One example of this is that growing number of congregations with two exceptionally competent preachers on the payroll. One is the "regular" preacher at two worship services on forty weekends every year. The second is the "regular" preacher at the other two worship experiences on forty weekends every year. On two or three or four weekends, each will preach at all four services. The big problem with that design is the shortage of highly competent preachers.

One implication for denominational leaders with two to five congregations in the same general community is to affirm both choice and quality as criteria in congregational planning on purpose, identity, role, and ministry. Frequently this abundance of congregations now carrying the same denominational label is the product of one or two denominational mergers consummated back in the days when that was a popular goal. A common result is two church buildings, each now carrying the same denominational label, within a few blocks of each other.

Once upon a time conventional wisdom urged a merger of the two congregations.[1] An alternative was to urge each congregation to develop an identity as a geographical parish. (This was before the widespread ownership of private automobiles.)

A more creative alternative for the twenty-first century is to begin by affirming choices. From a denominational perspective, this can be summarized by this statement: "Our goal is to offer people five (or six or four or three) choices. We are encouraging congregation A to identify itself as an evangelical high commitment church (see chap. 1). We are encouraging congregation B to sharpen its identity as a liberal church with a strong emphasis on issue-centered ministries. We are encouraging congregation C to become a seven-day-a-week church with a diverse program. We are encouraging congregation D to affirm what it is already practicing as an extended family that emphasizes caring, intimacy, healthy one-to-one relationships, and serving those who prefer a smaller-size congregation. We are encouraging congregation E to expand its present role, centered on nontraditional worship, contemporary Christian music, drama, and lay participation. We also expect all five will serve people from a ten- to fifteen-mile radius, that each will project a distinctive identity, and that each will build a professional staff that is consistent with that identity and role."

From a denominational perspective, that approach is consistent with the goal of seeking to serve people from a broad slice of the theological spectrum. From a congregational perspective, that statement can be consistent with affirming local traditions, strengths, and assets and building on those positive characteristics.

The dumbest reaction to this discussion of quality comes from those who believe quality and quantity are incompatible goals. The typical defensive statement resembles this: "The reason we are a small church is that we place a higher priority on quality than on quantity. We don't want to play the numbers game."

This can be an appropriate explanation if the goal is to nurture high-quality interpersonal relationships in a small congregation that resembles an extended and loving family.

If, however, the focus on quality is in worship, music, preaching, and teaching, and the quality is raised to a competitive level, that small congregation probably will attract hundreds of newcomers. People today are attracted by high-quality worship, by high-quality teaching ministries, and by high-quality preaching. That explains why huge numbers of Americans drive twenty to fifty minutes to church every week. Quality and quantity are compatible goals.

The most profound implication of this contemporary demand for both choice and quality is now being discussed by many people concerned with public schools and/or higher education in America. As the public universities in the United States grew in size in the 1945–75 era, many were not able to maintain a high-quality educational environment. Quality was sacrificed for quantity.

As William Glasser and others have pointed out repeatedly, this is largely an issue of leadership.[2] The responsibility of the leaders is to see that choices are increased, but not at the expense of quality. This places an unprecedented burden on pastors, senior ministers, and governing boards.

It is much easier and far less stressful to function as a small congregation in which institutional survival replaces outreach at the top of the priority list, in which caring is perceived as more important than choices, in which interpersonal relationships constitute the primary glue that binds the people together, in which a higher value is placed on spontaneity than on a long time frame for planning, in which tradition is more influential than creativity in planning for Christmas Eve and other special events, and in which funerals draw bigger crowds than are attracted by a musical concert.

Which road do you want to take into the twenty-first century?

7.

A New Generation of Young Adults

Forty years after graduating from high school, Ed Janko compared two high school yearbooks. One was the 1949 yearbook from his graduating class. The other was the 1989 yearbook from the high school in which he had taught for the past thirty-three years. He summarized the messages communicated by these yearbooks with a provocative comment. His graduating class of 1949 clearly believed in school. The graduating class of 1989 did not.[1]

In reflecting on the contents of these two yearbooks, this veteran English teacher lifted up several other generational differences. Most of the members of that class of 1949 had been born back in 1931–33. They viewed themselves as preparing for adulthood in an adult-owned and operated world. The yearbook conveyed images of serious, future-oriented, and orderly young people posing as "apprentices to their parents." These were the teenagers who a few years later were given the label "the silent generation."

The seniors of 1989 were drawn largely from the babies born in the 1971–73 era. The only obvious point of commonality was that each class represented a low point in this nation's birth curve. Earlier in 1921, for the first time in American history, the number of live births exceeded 3 million. That total was not reached again until 1943, but in 1933 a twentieth-century low was reached when only 2.3 million babies were born in the United States. That was Ed Janko's generation. After a two-year drop in 1944 and 1945, a new record was set in 1946, when 3,411,000 live births were recorded. During the next two decades, from 1947 through 1966, the number of live births in this country ranged between 3.6 million and nearly 4.3 million. After six more years of a gradual decline in births (due in part to the birth control pill and in part to the low number of births between 1929 and 1945), the nadir was reached in the 1973–76 era, when the total number of live births in this country ranged between 3.1 and 3.2 million. By 1985 the total was back up over 3.7 million and in 1989, for the first time in a quarter century, the total exceeded 4 million.

That second yearbook Ed Janko studied was produced by high school students who were born just before the most recent bottom of that birth curve.

A New Generation

Another perspective is to move from statistics on births to generational theory. Ed Janko and his classmates represented the generation born in the 1929–42 era. That generation not only believed in school, but it also believed in the value of institutions.

The students pictured in that 1989 yearbook came from the generation born in the post-1968 era, two generations removed from Ed Janko's "Depression babies" subculture.[2] In his brief essay, Janko observes that the members of his graduating class of 1949 were a part of the institutional culture of their day. They not only believed in school, but they were prepared to go forth and fulfill the role of "torchbearers of the traditions and values" of that culture as well. The class of 1989 had created its own culture that was "largely divorced from what school was all about."

High school yearbooks are but one of many signs and symbols that suggest that the babies born in the post-1968 era represent a new generation. Back in the mid-1980s the armed forces had to make substantial changes in their orientation and training programs in order to turn recruits into soldiers, sailors, marines, and airmen. The United States Army found it had to discharge one-fourth of all enlistees (and nearly one-half of those without a high school diploma) despite carefully designed screening procedures in recruiting.

By the late 1980s, civilian employees, college and university teachers, law enforcement officials, social workers, youth ministers, college chaplains and campus ministers, landlords, pastoral counselors, admissions directors in theological seminaries, and policy makers in the entertainment industry were beginning to recognize that about 70 percent of the members of this post-1968 generation represented a new breed of young adults.

How Come?

Before moving on to discuss a few of the characteristics of this new generation, it is necessary to return one more time to that veteran high school teacher, Ed Janko. What produced this new generation? Janko comments that after his generation left high school, they opted for a vastly different life-style for their children. He writes that a "utopian vision" caused his generation to accept "long hair, easy sex, drugs, perpetual adolescence, and life-as-entertainment" as the new way of the world. He refers to the "show business" atmosphere that is the theme of that 1989 yearbook.

In simple terms, who produced this new generation who are now the young adults of 1999? One answer is their parents. The other is the American culture of the 1970s and 1980s. The generations who themselves were born in the 1880–1910 era produced the national, business, governmental, educational, and religious leaders who were born in the pre–World War II era—the Ed Jankos of yesterday's high school teachers. The generations born in the 1930–50 era gave birth to most of the high school graduates of 1989. The high school graduates—and dropouts—of the 1984–99 era are the young adults of 2001.

Who Are They?

While it is too early to be able to offer a definitive description of this new generation born in the 1969–83 era, it appears that approximately one-third display a closer resemblance to their grandparents—the 1915–28 generation—than they do to their peers.

The traditional churches with a conventional approach to ministry usually can attract a large proportion of this 30 percent slice of today's high school youth and young adults. A common approach is to (a) build the ministry with teenagers around an attractive personality who is assisted by a couple of volunteers and (b) write-off the other two-thirds of the high school population. The typical twenty-three-year-old from this one-third of the young adult population can be integrated into the adult programming of that congregation if a serious effort is made to listen and to be responsive to what is heard.

What about the other two-thirds of this generation? One beginning point is to understand a few of the differences between them and older generations—who usually "run" the church.

First, this new generation does not believe in school, as Ed Janko pointed out, and they do not believe in institutions in general. That was a lesson taught them in their formative years. They learned and retained it.

Second, they have been reared in a culture that places immediate satisfaction above deferred gratification. One evidence of this is automobile ownership. A second is the importance of grades. A third is the increasing proportion who engage in sexual intercourse at an early age.

Third, they tend to create and live in their own subculture rather than to affirm and accept an inherited subculture.

Fourth, the majority of this generation who are employed during the school year see work as the center of their life. In Ed Janko's day, most of the students in high school and college saw academic classes as the center of their environment. Next to that was an array of extracurricular opportunities, including competitive sports. In third or fourth or fifth place were family or work or personal possessions or hobbies or church or some other activity or organization.

Today, for many high school and college students, the center of the universe is a job. In second place may be personal possessions. (This can be seen in the college and university dormitories constructed in the 1950s that have had to be rewired to accommodate the electrical appliances students now bring to school.) For a few, competitive sports are in the center of the universe. For many of today's teenagers, the youth gang is at the center of life. For others, their role as consumers is at the top of the priority list.

Fifth, when asked where they see an emphasis on quality in their world, most of the members of this post-1968 generation identify (a) the fast-food restaurant where they work, (b) competitive sports, (c) band, (d) automobiles, (e) other extracurricular activities, (f) a particular teacher, (g) clothing, (h) advanced placement classes in high school, (i) jewelry, and (j) other personal possessions. Home, classroom work, and church are rarely mentioned.

Sixth, unlike their parents, who lived in a world where people were classified by age and grade, today's teenagers tend to place greater weight on lines of demarcation based on (a) commonalities of race, nationality, ethnicity, and language; (b) religion; (c) use or non-use of alcohol, tobacco, and other drugs; (d) social class; (e) personal income; (f) home environment; (g) kinship ties; (h) culture; (i) grades in school; (j) dress; (k) ownership of an automobile; or (l) gang membership rather than on age or grade in building their friendship circles.

One part of the explanation for this, of course, is that a far larger proportion of today's teenagers are in very large and anonymous high schools than was true of Ed Janko's generation.

Seventh, completing an assignment is a lower priority with this generation than was the pattern with their parents' generation.

Today's youth and young adults are less task-oriented and more consumer-oriented than were their grandparents. Eighth, and this is of profound significance to the churches, they have been reared in a culture in which music and pictures are more popular channels of communication than are printed words. This is the MTV generation, not another typographic generation.[3] A nine-year-old often is able to name twice as many brands of alcoholic beverages or cigarettes as presidents of the United States.

Ninth, two-thirds of the members of this generation display less acceptance of personal responsibility for the consequences of their actions.

Finally, this generation tends to be in poorer health than their parents were at the same age, to be more likely to be obese, to score lower on verbal skill examinations, to display less respect for other persons and for the property of others, to reflect less respect for people who acquire authority by virtue of office, and, in many areas of life, to be both more conservative and more tolerant than earlier generations.

Employers, colleges and universities, military organizations, churches, voluntary associations, political parties, retailers, providers of entertainment, newspaper publishers, radio and television stations, service clubs, landlords, public agencies, restaurant owners, and automobile manufacturers all have found it difficult to earn and retain the loyalty and support of this new generation. This is a new and different generation from which the churches will be drawing their leaders by the end of the first quarter of the twenty-first century.

Between Now and Then

For those congregations not yet ready to welcome this post-1968 generation, four comments need to be offered as these leaders bid farewell to more and more of their members born before 1930 and seek to reach adults born after 1955.

First, to the surprise of many, that generation born in the 1956–68 era has been coming back to church in remarkably large numbers. While the older members of this generation will soon be identified as "middle-aged" rather than as young, this generation has very high visibility in those congregations that (1) place a premium on quality in everything from preaching to the nursery to meeting rooms to internal communication, (2) offer choices to people, (3) provide a strong and meaningful teaching ministry for adults, (4) find a place for contemporary Christian music and drama in corporate worship, (5) challenge people with high expectations, and (6) are open to creativity and innovation.

Second, two statistics are worth examining. In 1950, 71 percent of all Americans age eighteen and over were married, an all-time high for this country. By 1990, that proportion had dropped to 57 percent, an all-time low for this country. It may be wiser to focus on households rather than on couples in conceptualizing new ministries.[4]

Third, the demand for meaningful adult Bible study by this generation born in the 1956–68 era may be the most attractive single entry point open to churches seeking to reach this group of younger adults.

Fourth, except on issues related to sex, marriage, and divorce, this generation tends to be comparatively conservative. The churchgoers from this generation are more likely to be found in theologically conservative and in high commitment liberal churches rather than in low expectation liberal parishes.

What Are the Alternatives?

At about a quarter to eight on a beautiful evening in October, the person chairing the Long Range Planning Committee at First Church was asked to give his report to this special congregational meeting at First Church. To the surprise of many, nearly a hundred adults were in attendance.

"This is the first of two reports our committee plans to present," began this attorney, who had joined First Church in 1978 and was now a widely respected and influential leader.

69

"Tonight we want to offer our diagnostic report on the state of this church. We want you to feel free to ask questions at any point in the discussion. In about four months we will ask for a second special meeting of this congregation at which time we expect to present a plan of action."

During the next twenty minutes, this respected volunteer leader used a series of charts and graphs projected on a large screen to point out that during the past ten years (1) the average attendance at worship had dropped from 485 to 319; (2) the average attendance in the children's division of the Sunday school was down by 48 percent, in the youth division it was down by 61 percent, and attendance in the adult classes had dropped by 29 percent; (3) the size of the chancel choir had shrunk from 38-40 voices to 28-32 voices on the typical Sunday morning; (4) the number of circles in the women's organization had decreased from nine to three; (5) the median age of the confirmed membership had climbed from 44 to 53 years; (6) the percentage of confirmed members past age sixty had doubled; (7) the number of new confirmed members received had declined from an average of 86 annually for the period eight to ten years ago to an average of 27 for each of the past three years; (8) the amount of money in the reserve fund had dropped from $88,700 ten years ago to $9,310 today; (9) attendance in the Vacation Bible School had plummeted from 133 children ten years ago to 42 this past summer; (10) the number of adults in weekday and weeknight Bible study groups here at the church has dropped from a weekly average of 126 ten years ago to zero; (11) the death rate has climbed from an average of one death per one hundred members ten to twelve years ago to an average of three member deaths per one hundred confirmed members over the past three years; and (12) for the past five years this congregation has lost an average of three members for every one new confirmed member received.

When the attorney paused to solicit questions, one of the newer members said, "I wonder if our pastor would like to comment on what you have told us."

"My initial response is to plead 'Not guilty, your Honor,' " joked the obviously nervous senior minister who had arrived seven years earlier. "I feel like I have been listening to an indictment of my ministry by an exceptionally able prosecuting attorney."

"Please do not take this personally," interrupted the chair of the committee. "This was not intended to be an indictment of your performance. All we are trying to do this evening is present the facts to back up our diagnosis. Our committee has concluded that (a) as a congregation we are growing older and smaller, and (b) we appear to have lost our ability to attract and keep younger adults in general and especially younger families. Our next step is to design an action plan to reverse the trends we have presented this evening."

"I agree that the statistics you have presented are pretty depressing," conceded the pastor, who had remained standing during the attorney's interruption, "but they don't tell the whole story. From the day I arrived seven years ago, the board and I have agreed that our primary emphasis should be on quality, not quantity, and I think we have continued to move in that direction. While our numbers are smaller, we have an exceptionally loyal core of members who continue to be the backbone of this congregation. We have had a lot of members move away, and that explains the shrinkage in the size of our choir, but it is still by far the best choir in town. We do have difficulty in enlisting volunteers to teach, and that explains some of the drop in our Sunday school attendance, but Sunday school attendance is down in nearly every church in our denomination. The heart of our problem, as I see it, is due to three factors. First, there weren't many babies born back in the 1965–80 period, and that's why we have a comparative shortage of young adults in our whole society. Second, they're marrying later in life, and third, many are postponing the birth of that first baby."

"What do you propose we should do?" asked another member.

"I think we need to be patient, we need to keep on doing the best we know how to do, and one of these days you will see a lot of young families here. All we have to do is wait until they're married and have a couple of kids, and they'll be coming back to church," replied this fifty-four-year-old minister. "These things run in cycles, and one of these days we'll be short of space in our Sunday school."

What should this congregation do as it looks ahead to the twenty-first century? This is still a large and strong congregation. If the average attendance at worship is used to measure size, this church ranks among the top 6 percent in size in all of American Protestantism. For the first nine months of that calendar year, member contributions came to $288,400 and expenditures were $276,900, so the financial base is strong. A $250,000 renovation program was completed three years earlier, so the property is in excellent condition. That also explains that $79,300 shrinkage in the reserve fund, which was used to make up the difference between the $170,000 raised in the capital funds appeal and the actual cost of the renovation program. While several leaders, including the attorney chairing the Long Range Planning Committee, believe a change in ministerial leadership is overdue, most of the deeply unhappy people have left. Complacency, not discontent, is the dominant mood among the members.

This large and institutionally strong congregation can choose from among at least sixteen alternatives as it looks forward to the next few years.

1. It may continue to grow older and smaller. For many of the older longtime members, this is a comfortable choice. Caring, intimacy, simplicity, and continuity with the past promise more comfort than do change, anonymity, complexity, and discontinuity. A genuine crisis appears to be at least five, and probably ten, years away.

2. Rely on the denominational loyalty of newcomers to that community to bring in the replacements needed to remain on a plateau in size. Just because that has not worked in recent years does not mean it never will again.

3. Create and implement a plan to identify and court newcomers

to the community and pilgrims leaving other churches who might find this low-expectation congregation to be what they are seeking.

4. Seek to attract people from those two post-1955 generations who do not have any active church relationships and convert them to the culture of this low-expectation, complacent, and institutionally comfortable congregation.

5. Seek to build up an endowment fund of at least $3 million from bequests from the longtime and loyal members. The income from those investments could mean a financial crisis may be at least two or three decades away.

6. Hope that the adult children of today's members who have moved away will return and join this congregation.

7. Offer two different worship experiences on Sunday morning, one with music and sermons designed for those who prefer a traditional presentation approach to the worship of God and one designed for those who prefer a contemporary participation approach (see chap. 9).

8. In addition to those two choices on Sunday morning, add a Saturday evening worship experience designed for and by the older members of that post-1968 generation.

9. Affirm that worship and preaching can and should be good theater (see chap. 9) and implement that concept in designing one of the two (or two of the three) Sunday morning services. Utilize a show business approach to reach that MTV generation.

10. Greatly expand the teaching ministry and design the new weekday and weeknight classes, as well as all new Sunday morning classes, to serve as entry points for newcomers from those two younger generations of adults with special emphasis on reaching members of that 1956–68 generation.

11. Move from a low-expectation, voluntary association style of congregational life to a high-expectation covenant community style (see chap. 1).

12. Transform what is now largely a Sunday morning congregation into a seven-day-a-week program church by creating new classes, new worship services, new mutual support groups, new experiences, new music groups, new promotional events, and new opportunities for volunteers to be doing outreach ministries. These new classes, groups, and the like could serve as attractive entry points for new generations of members of all ages.

13. Raise the quality of all facets of the present program on the assumption that quality is far more important than style in attracting new generations. The assumption is valid, but the prescription is exceptionally difficult to implement! It requires a very high level of competence, determination, creativity, persistence, and hard work.

14. Move from what appears to be a middle-to-the-left point on the theological spectrum to a right-of-center or evangelical position. This will work only if it is 100 percent authentic and probably would require a replacement of all program staff and several volunteer leaders.

15. Conceptualize this as a congregation of congregations and systematically create a variety of entry points for newcomers from among these younger generations. One such entry point could be ministries with young single-parent mothers, another with those who want to be a member of a men's and boys' chorus, a third for childless young couples, a fourth for those who enjoy weekend or weeklong bicycle trips, a fifth for devotees of contemporary Christian music, a sixth for first-time parents, a seventh for those interested in creating and acting out the dramatic skits used on every Sunday morning to communicate the theme of that worship service, an eighth that is organized to help alleviate world hunger, a ninth that is organized as a support group for the weekday nursery school, and a tenth that helps to staff a hospice for those who know they are terminally ill but prefer not to die in a hospital.

16. Create a strategy that would combine two or three of these possibilities into one grand design.

Like thousands of other congregations that flourished with the loyalty and support of Ed Janko's generation, this church has been growing older and smaller. The easy alternative is to watch passively as that continues and hope that next year will be 1955. A more realistic, and far more demanding, alternative is to operate on the assumption that the twenty-first century is just ahead and make the changes required to reach new generations.

8.

WHERE ARE THE YOUNGER MALES?

During the first half of the twentieth century, when denominational structures were becoming increasingly influential, a convenient system for classifying churches was by denominational affiliation. During the quarter century following World War II, as urbanization became a highly influential trend, a useful classification system divided churches into two groups, rural and urban. The basis for this can be documented by a single set of statistics. In 1940, 43 percent of the 131.7 million residents of the United States lived in rural areas. By 1990 that proportion had shrunk to 23 percent of the 249 million counted in that census.

During the last half of the twentieth century, more and more observers of the ecclesiastical scene decided that the most meaningful classification was by theological stance. This perspective was popularized in 1972 by Dean Kelley's insightful book analyzing why the conservative churches were growing.[1]

In simple, pragmatic terms, the most widely used classification system in the United States has been and still is based on the race, nationality, language, or ethnicity of the members. Among the more widely used examples of this are such terms as "Swedish Lutheran" or "Black Baptist" or "Cuban Methodist" or "Korean Presbyterian" or "Dutch Reformed" or "Filipino United Church" or "Latino Assemblies."

The twenty-first century may bring a new system for classifying churches. This new system can be summarized by a simple brief question: "Which churches are reaching the men born after 1955?" How will that question be answered in the year 2025?

Going back to the 1950s, the available data suggest that in most of the mainstream Protestant denominations, about 52 to 55 percent of the adults and youth at worship on Sunday morning were female. This reflected the gender ratio of the population of America in the era. In 1950, 51 percent of all Americans age fourteen and over were female, up from 49 percent in 1930. In 1990 that proportion had climbed to 52 percent female for all Americans age fourteen and over.

By 1990, however, in the vast majority of the congregations affiliated with the old mainstream Protestant denominations in America, women accounted for 58 to 80 percent of the adults in worship on the typical Sunday morning. In hundreds of small-town and rural Anglo congregations and in many black churches, women outnumbered men in worship by a two-to-one to a five-to-one ratio.

Why?

This is not the place to attempt to offer an exhaustive analysis of that changing pattern. Even a superficial review, however, reveals that in most congregations (1) the number of attractive entry points for women exceeded the number of equally attractive entry points for men (examples include the women's organization, the choir, teaching, nurturing, and the choice of hymns), (2) the preaching often was designed for a female audience, (3) the pastor often was more comfortable with women than with men, (4) denominational resources often were designed for use by women rather than by men, and (5) the teaching ministry often was oriented toward women and children, not toward adult males.

Where Are the Women?

Another perspective for looking at this issue is to reflect on the characteristics of the congregations in which Sunday morning attendance usually is at least 60 percent female. The congregations that are predominantly female tend to display one or more of these characteristics: (1) they were founded before 1960 and/or recently have been shrinking in size; (2) they function as caring communities with a strong emphasis on taking care of one another and helping hurting people; (3) they display a theologically liberal stance; (4) they are affiliated with a numerically declining denomination; (5) they place a strong emphasis on issue-centered ministries; (6) they include a large proportion of widowed women, but few widowed men; (7) they draw most of their members from among people born before 1940; (8) they are composed largely of black members; (9) they are located in a rural setting or in the inner city; (10) they have experienced a series of brief pastorates during the past quarter century; (11) they are served by a minister who was reared by his or her mother and/or never enjoyed a healthy father-child relationship while growing up; (12) they are served by a pastor who holds at least one earned academic degree beyond college; (13) their pastor prefers a nondirective style of leadership—this is preferred by many women, while men tend to display a preference for the pastor who is willing to function as an initiating leader; (14) a high priority has been given to opening up every leadership role and office to women; (15) they display a strong member orientation rather than a strong outreach emphasis; (16) they place a high priority on taking good care of the pastor; and (17) most of the mutual support or self-help or recovery groups are designed in response to the hurts and needs of women.

What Are Some Clues?

While it is impossible to offer an accurate forecast of what American Protestantism will be like in the year 2025, several clues are now available that suggest what may happen.

The most obvious clue is that adult males are disappearing from most of the older mainstream Protestant congregations.

A second clue is that those worshiping communities that include a disproportionately small number of adult males come in large numbers from among the churches organized before 1960. Perhaps one way to attract larger numbers of younger males would be to encourage them to help pioneer new churches.

Men also can be found in larger proportions in those congregations in which a conscious and deliberate effort is made to design the sermon for right-brained adults in general and for men in particular. This deliberate approach, of course, leaves that preacher vulnerable to charges of sexism.

Two other patterns that disturb many ministers, both female and male, are that adult males can be found in disproportionately large numbers in (1) theologically conservative congregations that project high expectations of all members and (2) congregations that exclude women from policy-making positions for lay volunteers, such as elders, deacons, or trustees.

For many denominational leaders, the most distressing part of this trend is the small numbers of men from that post-1968 generation who are enrolling in the denominationally affiliated theological seminaries. That, however, is a subject beyond the scope of this chapter (see chaps. 7 and 13), but it may be a clue to the future of several mainline denominations.

Perhaps the most interesting clue is based on an assumption that has limited support. This assumption declares that during the twentieth century many trends that affected Anglos first gained high visibility among black Americans. Trends used to illustrate this assumption include (1) the migration of rural residents in large numbers to metropolitan areas, (2) the demand for equality without regard to race or gender, (3) the pattern of couples living together without first going through a formal wedding ceremony, (4) the problem of young men encountering greater difficulties in finding meaningful employment than was the pattern for their fathers, (5) the emergence of economic barriers to achieving the American dream of home ownership, (6) the growing proportion of husbands with a lower annual income than that earned by their wife, (7) the increasing proportion of babies born to unwed mothers, (8) the growing proportion of adult children who return to live with their parents, (9) the conclusion by teenagers that high school has little relevance to their future, (10) the attraction of the charismatic or Pentecostal expression of Christianity, (11) the importance of music in corporate worship, and (12) the gradual disappearance of younger males from Sunday morning worship.

While this is far from an exhaustive list, it does raise a pair of provocative questions. First, should what has been happening among black Americans be described as a leading indicator for Anglo America? Second, if so, what can be learned from where black men are appearing in large numbers in black churches? If Anglos eventually do follow patterns set earlier by blacks, it may be instructive to look at where black men can be found in church on Sunday morning.

A recent report on this issue pointed out that black men tend to be found in black congregations that (1) are not closely identified with any of the traditional black denominations, (2) emphasize orthodox Bible teaching, (3) aggressively encourage black men to marry and to accept full responsibility for their family, (4) give high visibility to the role of men in the church, and (5) act out the assumption that the gospel of Jesus Christ can transform lives.[2]

The black congregations that display all five of these characteristics often report that 40 to 50 percent of their adult worshipers are male, compared to 15 to 30 percent in the typical black church.

The white churches of today that report a large proportion of men among the worshipers on Sunday morning usually (1) are not identified with one of the mainstream Protestant denominations and include many men who were reared in another religious tradition[3]; (2) emphasize orthodox or traditional Bible teaching; (3) give high visibility to the role of younger men in leadership roles, including the teaching ministry (they model for male youth that church is a respectable place for adult males); (4) enjoy the leadership of a pastor who is an initiating or transformational leader; (5) were founded since 1970 or recently relocated to a new site; (6) offer men a variety of opportunities to express their creativity through nonverbal skills; (7) create all-male enclaves such as boards, classes, choirs, committees, and retreats; (8) offer a systematic program designed to enable men to articulate their faith; (9) challenge men to be evangelists; (10) display a clear goal-orientation in defining their role—these churches are *not* drifting from one year into the next; (11) act out the assumption that the gospel of Jesus Christ can transform lives; and (12) design worship services that include (a) hymns and songs that men feel comfortable singing, (b) highly visible roles for young adult male volunteers, (c) a twenty-five- to fifty-minute sermon designed for right-brained, visually oriented listeners, and (d) an adult choir or instrumental group that is at least 40 percent male.

That twelve-point list is not offered as a formula for reaching adult males in the twenty-first century. It is offered here only to underscore the central thesis of this chapter. The number-one line of demarcation in American Protestantism in the twenty-first century may turn out to be gender, but today both black and Anglo congregations are demonstrating why that need not become a self-fulfilling prophecy.

9.

WORSHIPING WITH NEW GENERATIONS

When a new independent and theologically conservative congregation was launched in a small town in Iowa in the late 1920s, the founders formulated a series of rules that were to be followed by anyone who wanted to join that new fellowship. The emphasis was largely on prohibited behavior. Among the many barriers to membership that were articulated were the use of tobacco or alcohol, swearing, wife-beating, dancing, bobbed hair on women, and attendance at the movies.

Fifty years later, a missionary couple returned from Africa to share their experiences with the members. Both had grown up in that congregation, and this church was the largest financial supporter of their ministry. The first Sunday morning after their return, they were asked to stand to be recognized during the worship service. They expressed their delight at being back home among friends and kinfolks. They also announced that after the Sunday evening service, they planned to describe their work and would show colored slides. Everyone was invited to attend.

That announcement took the elders by surprise, and they were clearly disturbed. Immediately after the benediction, they gathered for an emergency meeting. After nearly one hour of heated discussion, they agreed the missionary couple would be permitted to project their colored slides that evening, but it should be clearly understood that no one ever would be permitted to show, in that sacred building, "pictures that moved."

Fourteen years later, that decision was amended to permit the showing of videotapes, but the projection of motion pictures is still prohibited in that building.

From Service to Experience

This introduces one of the most significant changes that will affect the churches in the decades to come. This change is a new development, however, only in one slice of the churches on the North American continent. It has been highly visible for generations in Spirit-filled parishes, in many African-American congregations, and in a huge variety of Latino churches.

Motion and emotion are replacing passivity and the motionless presentation of the Gospel.

It is still easy to find those churches in which the preacher presents the sermon while the people sit passively, silently, and motionless. It is still possible to find churches in which the minister "presents the message" and tells the congregation when to pray, when to stand, when to sit, when to sing, when to be quiet, when to contribute money, and when to leave.

It also is still possible to find grandfathers and the occasional father who takes black-and-white still photographs of that new baby. Increasingly common, however, are 8mm movie cameras and camcorders. Parents and children appear to prefer pictures that move to still photographs.

Baseball or Soccer?

A useful analogy for describing this change is to look at the recreational preferences of eleven-year-olds. Back in the 1930s, baseball and softball were favorite summer sports of young boys—and of a smaller number of girls, but the girls were expected to watch, not play. Most baseball players spend a large portion of the game sitting on the bench or standing on the sidelines or standing in the field watching the pitcher and catcher throw the ball back and forth. Three or four or five fielders may go through an entire inning without touching the ball. For most of the players, baseball is a relatively passive, slow, and low energy sport. It resembles the corporate worship of God in thousands of churches. A few people have an extremely active role, but most are passive participants.

Baseball and softball trained the eleven-year-olds of 1935 for membership in churches where most of the men and all of the women watched a couple of men lead worship.

By the 1980s the favorite sport of millions of children was soccer. Soccer is a high energy and fast-paced participatory game in which most of the players, both male and female, frequently touch the ball. Soccer resembles the corporate worship of God in many of today's churches that have designed and implemented a participatory approach to worship.

What will the soccer playing eleven-year-olds of 1993 or 1999 look for as they seek a church in the year 2022 where they can come to worship God?

If one accepts the assumption that people do vote with their feet, one finds that younger generations of churchgoers apparently prefer participatory worship to the presentation style that dominated the scene in many Protestant traditions back in the middle of the twentieth century. Will that also be true in 2009?

What are the signs of this new approach to the corporate worship of God? The answer to that question can be communicated more effectively by experience than by words, but here are a dozen components of this affirmation of motion and emotion.

1. Liturgical dance is now a part of worship in more and more churches.
2. "Passing the Peace" has evolved from an awkward fad to a meaningful interchange among the worshipers.
3. Parishioners hugging one another and pastors hugging parishioners no longer are viewed as strange.

4. Instead of one person reading four or five announcements, each person with a message to be shared stands and delivers that announcement.

5. A two- to five-minute mini-drama that illustrates the central theme of the sermon is increasingly common.

6. Instead of asking worshipers to sing with their chins buried in their chests as they rely on a hymnal, more and more congregations project the words on a screen so people can sing with greater enthusiasm with their faces uplifted.

7. Instead of hiding behind the pulpit, more and more preachers are coming out of the chancel to deliver the sermon while walking among the people.

8. Instead of one person reading the Scripture in a boring monotone, that reading is shared by two or three persons who have memorized their lines.

9. Worshipers are motivated and encouraged to both laugh and applaud rather than to sit silently.

10. The person leading the congregation in public prayer often walks among the people to solicit their joys and concerns that will be included in the prayer of intercession.

11. The personal, and often emotional, testimony to the faith by a volunteer or two from among the members may be the most memorable part of that worship experience.

12. The choir comes down out of the choir loft to fill the aisles as the people hold hands during the benediction.

What once was correctly labeled a worship service has been transformed into a deeply moving, memorable, and meaningful worship experience.

From Preaching to Teaching

A parallel change is the rediscovery of the sermon as the primary channel in the teaching ministry of the worshiping community. Between the early decades of the nineteenth century and through the middle third of the twentieth century, the Sunday school gradually began to replace the sermon as the number-one expression of the teaching ministry. This was more widespread in the Methodist, Baptist, and Presbyterian traditions than in the more liturgical denominations, such as Anglican, Lutheran, and Episcopalian.

One product of this trend was the shortening of the sermon. "If you can't say what you have to say in eighteen minutes, you haven't spent enough time in preparation." Others argued a sermon should be no more than twenty or fifteen or twelve minutes in length.

Recent changes can be summarized by this six-part generalization. The larger the size of the congregation and/or the higher the skill level of the preacher as a communicator and/or the younger the worshipers and/or the stronger the emphasis on teaching sermons and/or the faster the pace of that worship experience and/or the greater the desire to reach adults who have not been actively involved in the life of any congregation for many years, the longer the sermon.

Sermons are getting longer. Today it is not unusual in the larger and rapidly growing congregations for the sermon to consume 35 to 75 minutes out of a 70- to 150-minute worship experience. By contrast, in scores of congregations that concentrate largely on reaching people born before 1935, the sermon may last for only 12 minutes in that 30- to 45-minute worship service. Obviously a higher level of competence in communication skills is required to hold the attention of people for 50 minutes than is needed for delivering a 12-minute message.

Perhaps the most distressing change in preaching can be traced back to the media in general and television in particular. Back in the 1950s the credibility of a public figure's speech was in the content. Did the content persuade the listener to agree with and support that message? Today the credibility is in the messenger, not the message. The visitor reflects while listening, "Does that preacher really believe what I am hearing?" If the listener has serious doubts about the preacher's credibility, a three-minute sermon probably is too long.

What Is Good Theater?

One of the difficult decisions facing the managers of supermarkets is how to sell gourmet cheese. One alternative is to hire a person who will spend the day standing at a display counter cutting cheese to order and wrapping, weighing, and pricing it for individual customers. Typically that person needs five hours to cut, weigh, price, and sell one wheel of cheese. The alternative is for the store to purchase it precut, vacuum wrapped, and with the price tag affixed to the package.

What is the tradeoff? It costs about 90 cents per pound to cut and wrap the gourmet cheese at the store, including the cost of labor, the wrapping film, and equipment. The pre-wrapped cheese costs 50 cents extra per pound over the price of the wheel of cheese, and it also offers the bonus of a longer shelf life than the store-wrapped cheese. What should the retailer do? Pre-wrapped or store-wrapped? Many choose the more expensive alternative, despite the shorter shelf life of the cheese.

Why? Because they are convinced that the drama and wrapping in-store with the accompanying perception of freshness is good theater.[1]

How did Ross Perot announce that he could be persuaded to become a candidate for the presidency of the United States? At a meeting of leaders from an existing political party? At a press conference? At a large outdoor political rally? No. Mr. Perot chose to make that announcement on the call-in television show of entertainer Larry King.

In terms of dollar value, what is the number-one export from the United States to the rest of the world? Agricultural products? Aircraft? Electronic equipment? Computer technology? No. The answer is entertainment.

One of the highlights of the 1992 presidential campaign was the sending of a present from the Vice President of the United States to the mythical baby of a famous television figure, Murphy Brown.

Several of the supermarket chains operate two sets of stores under different names. One is the giant warehouse where price and choice are the attractions. The other is the conventional supermarket where ambiance and showmanship are the attractions.

Shopping centers originally were designed to bring together dozens of retailers in one relatively small place for the convenience of shoppers. In recent years, scores of shopping centers have had to choose between losing money and transforming themselves into entertainment centers.

Once upon a time, those who evaluated restaurants for a television audience rated eating places on the quality of the food. Today several of the critics use two criteria. One is the quality of the food; the other is ambiance or theater.

The churchgoer who was bored by the sermon says to a friend on the way to lunch, "I didn't get a thing out of the sermon, but that anthem made it a worthwhile trip."

The syndicated religion writer George Plagenz once wrote a column explaining why preaching must be good theater. Plagenz declared, "Theater is something done with an audience in view. It must therefore be stimulating to the ear, the eye and the mind of the members of the audience." Plagenz points out that good theater usually includes passion, humor, feeling, and a message that speaks to the human condition.[2] Those also are the marks of good preaching.

Robert Randall makes the point that good preaching will convey a deep understanding of the human condition. Good preaching speaks to pain, struggle, and despair. Good preaching also offers hope, comfort, and joy. Good preaching speaks to that yearning to belong.[3]

Those also are the ingredients in good theater.

What Should You Do?

Should your congregation stick with the traditional solemn presentation approach to corporate worship that relies so heavily on oral communication? Or should you shift toward a greater emphasis on celebration, theater, drama, events, participation, motion, laughter, and music? What are the criteria you will use in making those decisions?

One answer begins with another question. Who are the people you are trying to reach so you can proclaim God's word to them and to make corporate worship a meaningful part of their lives?

A second response begins with (a) local congregational traditions and precedents; (b) the constraints imposed on you by the size, shape, and design of your physical facilities; (c) the gifts, skills, experiences, preferences, personalities, and creativity of your current ministerial leadership; and (d) the system of governance in your congregation—is it a permission-withholding or a permission-granting system?

A third, and far more important, criterion for making a decision is how has God spoken to human beings throughout history. One perspective lifts up God's communication through words. This perspective supports the presentation approach to worship. The other perspective is based on a belief that God spoke most powerfully to His children through events such as a burning bush, the parting of the Red Sea, the birth of a baby on Christmas Eve, the events on what we call Palm Sunday, the death and resurrection of Jesus, Paul's confrontation on the road to Damascus, Martin Luther's declaration that here stand I, and John Wesley's heartwarming experience at Aldersgate.

A fourth way of looking at what often is perceived as a divisive issue is to ask what is the foundation for worship here in this congregation.

In some parishes worship floats on a foundation of expository preaching, prayer, and praise. In others, the liturgy and the sacraments are the points of continuity.

In many small rural and central-city congregations, the crucial components of what makes Sunday morning work include friendship and kinship ties, one-to-one relationships of the people to a long-tenured pastor, caring, peer pressure, love, the weekly homecoming, singing, tradition, and participation.

At least a few churches explain that rationality is the distinctive component of their worship.

Many of the members of nontraditional congregations that are reaching large numbers of people born after 1955 insist that what makes worship into a meaningful and memorable experience for them is the combination of praise, learning, drama, comfort, preaching, music, joy, love, intercessory prayer, spiritual renewal, peace, theater, personalities, visual communication, laughter, understanding, passion, hope, and emotion.

A relatively new congregation in northern Indiana encourages this type of multifaceted worship in an eighty-minute experience with a coffee break in the middle.

As you plan for worship in your church in the twenty-first century, you also will be confronted with other questions that are becoming increasingly divisive. Take comfort. You are not alone in this struggle!

What Happened to the Hymnal?

In a large and rapidly growing Lutheran parish in the Midwest, the person coming to worship at either the second or fourth period on Sunday morning has two choices. One is to go upstairs in the beautiful Gothic sanctuary and worship following the traditional Lutheran liturgy. These worshipers sing, read, and pray from the clothbound green Lutheran book of worship and hymnal. It is a beautiful and meaningful worship experience that is enriched by the skilled contributions of an organist playing a pipe organ.

An alternative is to go down the steps to the fellowship hall and worship with approximately four hundred other people of all ages. In this service the worshipers sing from a book published by this congregation. Half of the nearly one hundred choices were written by members of this parish. The musical accompaniment on the typical Sunday morning in the fellowship hall is neither an organ nor a piano, but usually includes a keyboard, a guitar or two, a bass, and drums.

Once upon a time, it was possible to publish a hymnal on the assumption that "one size fits all." A parallel is that for many centuries footwear was designed to be worn on either foot. Today shoes often are sold in pairs, one for the left foot and one for the right foot.

In recent years, our culture has decided to recognize and affirm the differences among people. This can be seen most clearly in clothing, the efforts to make more buildings accessible to the disabled, that huge array of magazines and newsletters delivered by the Postal Service, the choices among cereals in the supermarket, the varieties of ice cream in the freezers in the grocery stores, cable television, and the music carried by various radio stations. Concurrently denominational loyalties are being eroded, and church shopping is becoming increasingly widespread.

Another influential part of the context for this discussion can be summarized under that rarely used word *exogamy*. It means marrying outside one's tribe or heritage. In 1990 the proportion of people in the United States who married outside their racial and/or religious heritage was more than double the rate in 1950. Thus black-white or Jewish-Protestant or Catholic-Protestant marriages create a challenge for those seeking to provide a meaningful worship experience for both partners in that marriage.

The result is that it is increasingly difficult to design a hymnal that will be acceptable to everyone. A common compromise has been to place in the pew rack the clothbound denominational hymnal and a paperbound songbook published by a parachurch organization.

Desk-top publishing and the emergence of central licensing companies have created a new alternative. More and more congregations are publishing their own hymnals. These often include (a) copyrighted hymns for which a fee is paid to a licensing company for reprint rights, (b) hymns that are now in the public domain, and (c) hymns, songs, and choruses composed by members of that congregation.

One other part of the background for this change is symbolized by the career of Thomas Andrew Dorsey, often called the father of the gospel song. During the 1930s Mr. Dorsey brought blues rhythms and showmanship into the churches, first in Chicago and subsequently throughout the nation.[4] The growing popularity of the music that came out of the black churches, out of charismatic and Holiness traditions, out of the African-American experiences, out of the Native American religious culture, brought to these shores by Latino and Asian immigrants, and from the new transdenominational churches has greatly enriched the choices available to churches today. This abundance means that no one hymnal can contain all of it.

Every congregation now can have a custom-designed hymnal created to reflect the preferences, creativity, tastes, traditions, and approaches to the corporate worship of God of that gathered community. This is an especially significant development for any congregation that (a) seeks to become a multicultural community and/or (b) welcomes adults who were reared in a different religious culture with a different musical heritage and/or (c) schedules three or four different worship experiences every weekend, but prefers to use the same hymnal at all of these services.

An increasingly popular alternative is the "chins up" approach to congregational singing that utilizes a projector, transparencies or slides, and screens on which the words are displayed. The "chins down" churches can use their own locally created and published hymnal. Those congregations with unusually strong denominational loyalties can use the hymnal published by their denomination. Each of these three alternatives will have a large following for at least the early years of the twenty-first century.

What Happened to the Organ?

If you meet all three of the following criteria, you may prefer to skip this section. What are these criteria? (1) You love organ music, (2) you hate contemporary Christian music—and may even consider that phrase an oxymoron, and (3) you are convinced the first year of the twenty-first century will be a carbon copy of 1951.

A front page article in the *Wall Street Journal* for October 1, 1992, highlighted two interesting trends. First, the sales of new home organs, as reported by the American Music Conference, were 13,300 in 1991. That total was down from 222,400 in 1977.

Second, well over one-fourth of those 1991 sales, and perhaps close to one-half of the 1992 sales, were made by one store in Port Richey, Florida. The owner offers a ten-week course to those who want to learn to play an electronic organ. Those who purchase a new organ receive a lifetime of free organ lessons. Most of the buyers are retirees, so that offer is not as generous as it first appears.[5]

A third national trend raises a provocative question. Why is the number of people studying organ dropping? Is it the absence of employment opportunities? Or is it a lack of interest by younger generations in mastering that musical instrument?

Finally, one more piece in this mosaic also can be introduced by a question based on this author's experiences. What is the closest to a guaranteed means of evoking a hostile response from among a large number of the participants in a workshop on challenges facing today's churches? A discussion on abortion on demand? Unilateral disarmament by the United States? The compensation of pastors? Homosexuality? The rise of the megachurch? The competitive pressures on the small rural church? Vouchers for children attending a private school? The decline of denominational influence? Racism? Egalitarianism? The conflicting expectations placed on theological seminaries? The role of the Sunday school? Sexism? Tithing? Evangelicalism? The role of the women's organization? The use of television by churches?

Each one of those usually will arouse debate that can escalate into a heated argument. The one issue, however, that always evokes strongly held feelings of dissent is the suggestion that organ music in church is no longer widely popular. A close second is any suggestion that a congregation might consider replacing those clothbound hymnals with an overhead projector and choruses. An attempt to implement those two possibilities could put a pastor in the unemployment lines in thousands of today's churches.

It is ridiculous, of course, to suggest that the organ is an obsolete musical instrument. Pipe organs will continue to be the primary musical instrument in scores of cathedrals for many generations yet to come. It also is still in great demand for funerals, for an occasional wedding, and still widely used in those congregations that focus their ministry on people born before World War II. It is an endangered species only in those congregations seeking to reach and serve individuals from the generations born after 1945 who do not have an active church relationship.

This raises two more questions. First, is this true? Will the organ completely disappear from the churches? The answer, of course, is no one knows. If the world does come to an end in the year 2000, millions of Christians will sing to the accompaniment of an organ in their last worship service here on earth. Likewise, if the average life expectancy of people born in the 1920s and the 1930s is extended to a norm of 120 years, the organ will be widely used in the year 2031, long after all copies of this book have been recycled.

Who killed it? That is an easier question to answer. Television in general and MTV in particular. If the MTV generation born after 1968 outlives their parents, and the MTV generation becomes the congregational leaders of 2005 to 2030, the organ may not be as popular in 2025 as it was in 1955.

What is the replacement for the organ? It is too early to tell, but it appears the answer will be a long paragraph, not one word. That paragraph now includes words such as guitar, band, keyboard, drums, violin, flute, bassoon, bass, orchestra, synthesizer, accordion, brass, and recorded tapes.

From Less to More

Finally, one of the most far-reaching changes in worship in many American Protestant congregations is in the frequency of Holy Communion. For some, this always has been a part of the corporate worship of God. For most, however, the trend has been from less frequent to more frequent. For some traditions the change is from quarterly back in the 1950s to monthly in the 1990s. In others, it is from monthly to weekly. In a few congregations that have made a special effort to welcome pilgrims reared in a Roman Catholic home, the change has been from monthly or weekly to daily.

This trend has disturbed those who believe the increased frequency has demeaned the significance of Holy Communion.

This change also challenged the tradition that the Lord's Supper can be administered only by the fully credentialed clergy. A growing number of the laity are now being authorized to carry out this responsibility. This change also has disturbed those who feel that this dilutes or undermines the meaning of ordination.

The other big change in Holy Communion has been from less open, or closed, to nonmembers to more open. As recently as 1950 it was common for congregations to communicate to visitors that Holy Communion was closed to all except (a) members of that congregation and/or (b) members of that particular religious tradition or denomination. Today the visitor is more likely to be welcomed by the announcement that this congregation practices open Communion.

This change in the frequency of Holy Communion also has produced another change that comes under the umbrella of from less to more. How does the congregation respond when one-third of the members insist on weekly Communion, one-third believe monthly is correct, and one-third prefer not to go to war over this issue?

A common compromise is to serve Holy Communion every Sunday morning at the first service and once a month at the second service.

A similar compromise also has been the prime motivation for changing from one to two worship services on Sunday morning. At one service the organ will be the musical instrument of choice. At the other service, the band will play.

Back in the 1950s, the primary reason for scheduling two worship services every Sunday morning was to solve the space problem. A decade later the primary motivation was to give people a choice of time. Today the primary justification may be to give the people a choice between two substantially different worship experiences. One may be a traditional presentation format with the organ, the denominational hymnal, Reverend A as the preacher, and the chancel choir as the distinctive components of that service. The other may be more of a participatory style with Pastor B preaching, a band, a paperbound songbook or an overhead projector with the words of the hymns or choruses projected on a screen, and a Christian rock group as the distinctive components of that experience.

While still relatively rare, another alternative is the early service designed for believers and a later worship experience on Sunday morning designed for searchers, seekers, shoppers, pilgrims, inquirers, and first-time visitors.

In other parishes, this matter of choice is simplified by scheduling concurrent services.

What if the father and the seventeen-year-old daughter prefer one service, and the mother and fifteen-year-old son prefer the other? One solution is to schedule them concurrently with one in the sanctuary and the other in the fellowship hall.

The preferences of today's people are gradually replacing local traditions, legacies inherited from those now in nursing homes and cemeteries, the design of the building, and denominational patterns as the most influential factors in designing worship experiences for new generations.

This does not happen easily! Opponents include those who would sanctify tradition, many of those born before 1940, a few members who paid for the hymnals "that are still like new," pastors who are overwhelmed by the idea of preparing two or three different bulletins every weekend, people who are convinced that the family that worships together will stay together, several dozen custodians and organists, a couple of the remaining charter members, the former pastor who moved back here after retirement, publishers of clothbound hymnals, and organ builders—and that is far from a complete list!

10.

MAKING MEMBERSHIP MORE MEANINGFUL

How do you define *member?*

One response to that question in American Protestantism has been to establish two categories of membership—baptized and confirmed. A second has been to use a similar two-stage sequence of baptized and communicant. A third has been to affirm only one initiatory rite and count those who have passed through that rite as members. That ritual may be identified as baptism, profession of faith, confirmation, confession of faith, or some parallel event.

A fourth system has been to divide all members into two categories—active and inactive. In some traditions, that division is between resident and nonresident. In others it is between participating persons and nonparticipating persons.

The least troublesome response has been to eliminate from the agenda any concept of local church membership. It would be presumptuous for sinful human beings to seek to identify who is a member of God's church. Only God can know who is a member of God's church. That eliminates the need for new member classes, programs designed to activate the inactive, or that distressing annual chore of "purging the membership rolls."

A growing number of congregations, as part of a larger strategy of moving back toward a high commitment identity (see chap. 1) utilize the concept of a *term membership.* The typical pattern is that all memberships automatically expire at midnight on December 31. Those who want to continue as full members for the new year sign a new covenant of membership for that coming new year. This can be a meaningful component of a New Year's Eve worship experience.

A few very high-commitment congregations have exceptionally high standards for becoming a full voting member, but make it easy for anyone to identify with and worship with that fellowship. Typically they also make it extremely easy for people to leave and offer a variety of support systems to reduce the pain, guilt, or regret that may be evoked by departure.

The Concentric Circle Approach

A response that is attracting an increasing number of adherents can be conceptualized as a series of concentric circles. The larger outer ring embraces everyone who seeks to be a part of that worshiping community. In some congregations all that is required is the request to have one's name placed on the mailing list. In others, repeated attendance places your name on that list. Normally this degree of inclusion is not accompanied by the privilege to vote in congregational meetings nor to hold office. It may, however, include the right to attend and to speak at congregational meetings. Common generic labels for those who are inside this big outer ring include worshipers or inquirers or constituents or friends or participants.

Entrance into the second largest circle is more difficult. This may require completion of a thirty-six- or forty-two- or forty-five- or forty-eight-week new member training program. It may require baptism or rebaptism or a profession of faith or a personal oral or written testimony of one's faith pilgrimage or an oral examination by the elders or a similar ritual. Passage into this second ring usually carries with it the privilege to vote at congregational meetings. It may also carry the right to serve as a worker (choir member, usher, volunteer in the kitchen, helper in a Sunday school class or vacation Bible school or part-time volunteer worker in the church office or janitorial assignments) but not as a teacher, leader, policy maker, counselor, greeter, or caller.

Those responsibilities are reserved for people who qualify to be within that smallest inner ring. Admission into this inner circle, which may not be formally defined or given high visibility, usually combines both objective and subjective criteria. A common one is the commitment to tithing. This commitment may simply require the annual turning in of a signed card stating that the signer will tithe one-tenth of next year's income. In other congregations, that commitment specifically declares that one-tenth of the signer's income will be returned to the Lord via the financial channels of that congregation.

In a growing number of congregations, entrance into that inner circle requires completion of a lengthy formal Bible study course and/or regular attendance at weekly worship and/or active participation in an organized Bible study and prayer group and/or completion of a program designed to help believers move on to become disciples and/or completion of a structured 60- to 120-hour specialized training experience designed to prepare one to fulfill the responsibilities of a teacher or greeter or counselor or policy maker or deacon or elder or evangelist or missionary.

The subjective criteria for entrance into this inner circle often include character, Christian commitment, a willingness to accept volunteer assignments, personality, competence, adherence to and support of the basic doctrinal statements of faith of that congregation, loyalty to the pastor, approval by other leaders, or experience.

Another Perspective

An institutional perspective of this issue of the definition of membership consists of a long line or spectrum. At one end of that spectrum are located those religious bodies that are clearly high-commitment covenant communities. High standards of both belief and behavior must be met to become and continue as a member of that covenant community. At the other end of that spectrum are the self-identified voluntary associations.

Typically these congregations project far fewer barriers to those who seek to become members. Some of the members were born into that congregation and may be regarded as "birthright Christians." Others came by letter of transfer. Many may have joined by a profession of faith that required assent to certain questions on religious beliefs, but was not reinforced by rigid performance standards. A person might take the vows of membership on one Sunday morning, return on only a dozen Sundays during the next decade, but still be listed as a member in good standing. These congregations usually have a cumbersome and restrictive procedure that makes it difficult to remove a person's name from the membership roll. By contrast, the high-expectation or covenant community churches often have a simple procedure that makes it easy to remove a person's name from the membership roll.

While it is rarely discussed in these terms, the churches at the voluntary association end of that spectrum often convey the impression that members are perceived as customers, rather than as part of a disciplined covenant community. A common expectation in the voluntary association model is that members are customers who must be courted, consulted, heard, pleased, heeded, informed, and obeyed. It is not unusual for the new minister to be advised that the top priority for the first few months of that new pastorate should be to "listen to those who pay the bills, call on the shut-ins, cultivate the pillars, and listen to the old timers." It is widely assumed that God speaks to these churches through the will of the majority (or sometimes even a highly articulate minority) rather than through set-apart leaders.

Consistent with this view of members as customers is a central characteristic of a voluntary association. This is the right of withdrawal. An individual may make a unilateral decision to terminate his or her membership, and that is the end of that relationship. By contrast, in the covenant community the termination of one's membership requires approval of the governing board, just as a parallel action is necessary to become a member.

It is not unusual for the congregations at the covenant community end of this spectrum to report that their worship attendance usually exceeds their total membership. At the voluntary association end of this spectrum, the average worship attendance-to-membership ratio usually is less than 50 percent and may be as low as 30 percent.

Scattered between the two poles of that spectrum are perhaps two-thirds of all the Protestant congregations in North America. New ones keep appearing at the covenant community end, while some of those at the voluntary association end dissolve, merge, or simply grow older and smaller with the passage of time.

During the twentieth century, American Protestantism has included two parades moving in opposite directions. One parade consists of those denominations and congregations that were created as high-commitment religious bodies. They now are composed largely of second-, third-, and fourth-generation Christians who gradually have been drifting toward the voluntary association end of this spectrum. The second parade consists of new and renewed covenant communities moving toward the high-commitment end of this spectrum as part of a larger strategy to reach and serve new generations of new Christians. Where is your congregation on that spectrum? Which direction is it headed?

Is Life Sequential?

In many of the newer congregations seeking to reach and serve inquirers, seekers, searchers, pilgrims, and new Christians, as well as in a growing number of revitalized churches, the answer to those two questions consists of two parts.

The first part is an unequivocal response, "We are moving toward the covenant community end of that spectrum!" The second half of their churches' response is "We begin with future members where they are on their faith journey today and encourage them to move toward that high commitment end of the spectrum."

Their strategy can be depicted as a six- or seven-stage sequence. In the first stage, the pilgrims, skeptics, seekers, searchers, and inquirers are warmly welcomed as worshipers, but no demands are placed on them. When these inquirers display the appropriate level of interest, they are invited to become part of a new study group that is designed to explore the Christian faith. This often is scheduled with weekly meetings for six to twenty-four months. After several months in this explorers' class, those who are interested are invited to move to stage three and become part of a new class for those who are interested in formally uniting with that congregation. The focus of these classes often ranges from an introduction to the Bible to a discussion of the history, doctrinal stance, role, and identity of this congregation to a review of the history of the Christian churches to a description of the organizational structure and group life of this congregation.

The "graduates" of that class consist of those who do request membership. Uniting with that congregation usually is not viewed as either a destination or even as a stage in this sequence. It is simply a gate through which one passes into stage four of this sequence.

For some of these pilgrims, stage four consists of an in-depth study of the Bible followed by stage five, which concentrates on doctrinal and faith issues. For others, that part of the sequence is reversed and stage four consists of the doctrinal and faith questions followed by that in-depth Bible study in stage five.

For those who accept the challenge, the sixth stage is the most intensive of all. This is the discipling program designed for those who seek to become active disciples of Christ. The most common statement by those who complete this stage is simply, "This has transformed my life." The seventh stage is, of course, ministry and service.

In many congregations teachers, policy makers, and other volunteer leaders are chosen only from among those who have completed the discipling stage of this sequence.

This approach to making membership more meaningful includes six critical assumptions. First, it is assumed that for many people life is sequential and that sequence includes a spiritual pilgrimage. Second, it is assumed that the ritual of receiving people as members does not automatically create disciples out of these new members. Third, formal membership should be conceptualized as a gateway, not as a destination. Fourth, the design recognizes that different people move at different paces on their pilgrimage of faith. Fifth, this congregation has an obligation to honor and to be responsive to the religious needs of people at all seven stages of this sequence. Finally, and perhaps most important, the primary responsibility for making membership meaningful to everyone rests on the leaders, not the members.

This sequential view of membership often arouses a strong dissent from (a) those who perceive the act of uniting with a congregation to be a destination, not a gateway, and (b) the self-identified "born-again Christians" who divide the population into two categories, born-again believers and nonbelievers.

What Is the Dominant Pattern Today?

What is the dominant pattern as American Protestantism moves into the third millennium? Is the parade moving toward the voluntary organization end of that spectrum larger than the parade moving toward the covenant community end?

The answer depends on what you count. If you count congregations, the larger parade appears to be moving toward the voluntary association end of that spectrum. If, however, you count younger churchgoers, the fast-growing parade is moving toward the covenant community approach to making membership meaningful.

What does your congregation plan to do to make membership more meaningful to people in the twenty-first century?

11.

HOW MANY INCOME STREAMS?

I n my opinion, if we can't expect to pay for it out of the offering plate, we shouldn't do it," urged Harold Barton, who chaired the finance committee at Bethel Church. "I don't have any serious problem with the three special offerings we receive every year. One goes for foreign missions, one for home missions, and one is to help fund the pensions of retired ministers. Those are all worthy causes, but I don't want to see us taking up two or three special offerings every Sunday!"

"I agree!" declared Jim Anderson. "There is a limit on how often we should ask our people for money. The worst image a church can have is that it's always begging people for money."

"That fits my philosophy exactly," commented the recently arrived pastor. "I believe we should go to the people once a year with a proposed budget and if the members approve it, that's it. If I could have my way, we would include all our mission giving in the budget and do away with all special offerings, but I guess that's not completely realistic."

"If every one of our members would tithe and return only half of that tithe to the Lord via the offering plate, we could do it," suggested Ed Matthews. "That would give us a lot bigger income than we now have and would enable us to cut out all special offerings and quadruple what we send to missions."

By the time that meeting came to an end, the members of the committee had agreed on a $26,300 budget for 1954. They estimated that receipts would include $25,000 in the tithes and offerings, another $800 in those three special offerings, $200 in the loose offering, and $300 from memorial gifts.

"That's not bad for a congregation that is now averaging 145 at worship," declared Harold Barton with an obvious sense of satisfaction over a job well done.

The year was 1953, and this conversation occurred during the preparation of the budget for Bethel Church for 1954.

Forty years later, Harold Barton's son, David, chaired the finance committee at Bethel Church. A loyal, life-long, conscientious member, David had spent at least twenty hours in preparation for this meeting. "Before we begin to look at all the requests for money from the various boards and committees, I believe we should try to reach agreement on our anticipated receipts. Last week I met with our pastor and our treasurer, Tim Ryan, who is sitting across the table from me now, in an effort to come up with some realistic estimates on our income for next year."

"What's the total you project for next year?" interrupted an eager member. "How much do you figure we'll have to work with next year?"

"Before I answer that," replied David Barton, "I would like to run through the various sources. We expect tuition, fees, and special gifts for our Early Childhood Development Center will come to $92,000. Given the current level of interest rates, I believe we can count on another $43,000 in income from our endowment fund. As you all know, we have scheduled a Miracle Sunday for the second weekend in May next year. The goal is to raise $115,000 to pay off the remainder of the mortgage from the remodeling program we completed five years ago. Thus far a total of 37 task forces, committees, and other groups have permission to conduct special appeals for missions. I expect they will average about $300 each, so that comes to about $11,000. The trustees are planning three special offerings for real estate improvements that come to $12,000. The various programs, besides our Early Childhood Development Center, for which we charge user fees, such as the new adult Bible study program, weekday child care, meals, vacation Bible school, and youth trips, should bring in at least $9,000. We can expect to have one national or international disaster for which our missions committee will schedule a special offering. That may bring in as much as $3,000. Our denomination is running a major capital funds appeal, and our quota is $17,000 per year for each of the next three years. We are projecting $181,000 in tithes and offerings and another $6,000 in loose offerings in the collection plate."

"Pardon my interrupting," said another member of that committee, "but how much of that $181,000 from our members comes in through the offering plates and how much through other channels?"

"I guess I'm in the best position to answer that," responded the treasurer, Tim Ryan. "Fifteen years ago, when I first became treasurer, the answer would have been most of it. This year it is less than half. Many of our largest contributors mail in a check once a quarter, several bring stock or bond certificates to the church office. Our second and third largest contributors always give us a check in mid-December to cover their pledge for the coming year. My guess is that next year most of that $17,000 for the denominational capital funds campaign and at least $100,000 of the regular giving by our members will come in to the church office rather than through the offering plates. Our daughter, who is the financial secretary of a big church in Cleveland, told me that less than a third of their total contributions come in through the offering plates. I don't know what to predict about Miracle Sunday next May, since we've never done that here, but I expect at least a third will come in directly to the church office rather than be placed in the offering plates."

"Satisfied with that answer?" asked David Barton. "If so, let me continue. We are projecting our bookstore will bring in a net profit of at least $3,000 next year. Finally, on the basis of our experience over the past few years, I believe we can project $9,000 in memorial gifts. We have a number of very attractive possibilities for memorials that have not yet been underwritten, so that may be a conservative estimate."

"Wow! If my addition is correct, that comes to a total of $501,000," exclaimed that impatient member who earlier had asked for a total figure for anticipated income. "That's a huge increase over this year, when our budget is for only $278,000."

"Yes, that's what it appears to be," cautioned David Barton, "but remember a lot of that projected income is already earmarked for how it will be used. Our Early Childhood Development Center will cost us about $115,000 next year, including utilities, custodial and secretarial services, and office expenses, so that $92,000 will simply cover part of that program's costs. That $115,000 from Miracle Sunday is earmarked for paying off our mortgage. We expect that most of the $17,000 for the denomination's capital funds appeal will come in the form of designated contributions. The $43,000 from the endowment fund is restricted to capital improvements, and I expect we'll use it toward buying the house next door that the trustees believe we must acquire. Likewise the $11,000 in special offerings for missions and the three appeals by the trustees also are earmarked for special purposes, as are nearly all memorial gifts."

"What do you expect in bequests next year?" inquired another member of the finance committee.

"That's something you can't budget," explained David, "but unless we are instructed to the contrary, all bequests go into the endowment fund. Income from that is restricted and can be used only for capital improvements or financing the first year costs of new ministries or for missions. During the past ten years we have received a total of $240,000 in bequests, which I have been told is about twice the average for a congregation of our size in this denomination. The main reason we have such a big endowment fund is that seventeen years ago we received a bequest of Coca Cola stock which included a restriction that it could not be sold for fifteen years. When we did sell it, that sale alone more than doubled the size of our endowment fund."

"If I understand what you're telling us, Dave, we as a finance committee really have control over the allocation of only a little over half of that nearly half million in our total income," commented another member.

"That's correct," replied David. "To be precise, we can budget the expenditure of $291,000 in projected income. The other $210,000 is earmarked and beyond our control. You also need to remember that $92,000 for the Early Childhood Development Center must go toward the cost of that program, so we really have approximately $200,000 over which we have discretionary control."

*   *   *

This pair of conversations illustrates several of the changes that have transformed the way congregations will be financing their life, ministry, and outreach in the twenty-first century.

The most obvious, and perhaps the most far reaching, change is the shrinking proportion of the total receipts that come in via the offering plate. In a rapidly increasing number of congregations that (a) offer an extensive weekday program and/or (b) enjoy significant income from investments and/or (c) rely on user fees, the proportion of total income that comes in via the traditional tithes and offerings is less than one-half of the total receipts.

A simple example and increasingly common practice is not a part of the financial picture at Bethel Church, but it is a growing trend: wedding fees. It is not uncommon today for congregations to have a two-level fee schedule for weddings. One fee covers everything from the custodian's services to a wedding consultant to honoraria for the minister and organist to a videotape of the ceremony made by that congregation's audio-visual department to use of the fellowship hall to candles. For members that fee may be $300 to $700 and substantially more for nonmembers. With two or three dozen weddings a year, that can add up to a significant amount of money. (Those who believe churches and ministers should not accept fees for weddings may want to define the line that isolates those services for which fees will be charged, such as weekday child care, from those for which no fee will be accepted.)

Overlapping this major point is that for a variety of reasons, one of which is tax considerations, more and more of the larger contributors are not placing their contribution in the offering plate. An obvious example of this change is the contributor who makes a gift in the form of stocks or bonds that have appreciated in value. Another is the growing trend that is represented by the member who, when preparing the annual income tax returns, takes the standard deduction every other year and itemizes deductions in the alternate year. Even more common is the member who mails in or drops off a check once a quarter or once a month to cover the contributions for that period.

Perhaps the least publicized change is represented by the fact that Protestant congregations in the United States now receive well over one billion dollars annually in bequests and legacies. Occasionally those funds are spent on operating or capital costs, but usually these bequests are invested, and only the income is used.

The magnitude of this trend is illustrated by the pastor who commented in early 1993, "While we should have done it a lot sooner, we created our foundation to receive bequests in 1978. We now have slightly over a million dollars in the foundation, but expect that will grow to at least six million during the next ten years."

This pastor's comment is a reflection of (a) the fact that the number of Americans age 65 and over doubled from 16.5 million in 1960 to 33 million in 1992, (b) the generation born back in the 1920s turned out to be the most churchgoing generation in American history, (c) Americans age 65 and over owned over $5 trillion in wealth in 1993, (d) slightly over 1.6 million of those mature adults will die annually during the 1990s, and (e) many of them loved their church and were encouraged to remember their church in their will.

In those congregations in which the income from bequests is invested, rather than used to balance the budget, this has long-term implications. That accumulated wealth can be a substantial source of income a few years down the road!

What Does This Mean?

While the financial picture at Bethel Church used to open this chapter may be an atypical pattern, it does serve as a useful beginning point. What can the typical congregation averaging 300 at worship in the year 2010 expect as it projects various income streams?

Tithes and offerings from members	40 to 90%
Loose offering and nonmember contributions	5 to 20%
User fees and grants from outside organizations for specialized programs	20 to 60%
Income from investments	5 to 20%
Memorial gifts	2 to 6%
Modest scale special offerings	5 to 1%
One large annual special appeal	15 to 30%
Unsolicited special gifts for designated purposes	5 to 2%
Sales of merchandise (books, etc.)	3 to 10%

In other words, it may be more meaningful to talk about income streams rather than simply to focus on tithes and offerings in projecting receipts. How many income streams does your congregation now enjoy? Should that number be increased? Which ones are you most comfortable with in terms of your theology, your philosophy of ministry, and your local traditions? Which new ones should be cultivated as you seek to broaden the financial base of your congregation for the third millennium?

12.

CREDENTIALS OR CHARACTER, COMMITMENT, AND COMPETENCE?

Four of the most critical issues facing American Protestantism in the third millennium have been largely ignored by most church leaders until recently. One is the changing role of denominations, which is discussed in chapter 14. A second, which is rarely discussed openly, is the gradual disappearance of adult males from literally thousands of congregations (see chap. 8). The third, which many are still reluctant to admit is a problem, is that the old systems for enlisting a new generation of seminarians are not working as well as they did in the 1950s (see chap. 13). The fourth, which may be the most widely ignored or resisted, is the fact that ordination does not even promise, much less guarantee, competence as a parish pastor. This raises an important question: What are the best criteria for evaluating candidates for ordination?

It may be helpful in reflecting on that question to look first at four significant trends.

Who Defines the Criteria?

Between 1890 and 1990 the number of Protestant congregations in the United States increased from 153,000 to an estimated 325,000—and the actual current total may be closer to 350,000. During that same period the population of the United States quadrupled from 63 million to over 252 million, while the number of Protestant congregations did not even triple. In 1890 there was one Protestant church for every

410 residents. A century later the ratio was one church for every 770 residents.

Back in 1890 nearly two-thirds of all Protestant churches placed the responsibility for ordination in a regional or national agency of the denomination. The six predecessors of what is now The United Methodist Church accounted for 49,500 of these 95,000 congregations that placed the responsibility for ordination in a denominational body. Nearly 9,000 were Lutheran, 5,000 were Protestant Episcopal, and another 16,000 were affiliated with one of the Presbyterian or Reformed traditions.

This meant that for 64 percent of the Protestant congregations in 1890, a denominational agency or committee defined the criteria for evaluating candidates for ordination. From 1810 to 1970 formal educational credentials became an ever more influential component of that process.

In 1990 approximately 135,000 of the 325,000 Protestant congregations in the United States placed the authority and responsibility for ordination in the regional or national offices of the denomination. That represents a drop from 64 percent to 42 percent. Today the majority of American Protestant congregations now place the authority for ordination in the congregation. This is part of the larger trend in the redefinition of the role of denominations and the response of churchgoers to those changes (see chap. 14).

Where Are the Bright Young Men?

One of the most widely articulated concerns in both Protestant and Roman Catholic circles is the sharp drop in the number of gifted young white males who are planning to become parish pastors. Fifty years ago the ranks of the clergy were filled with enthusiastic, bright, eager, and gifted young men.

Where are their counterparts today? First, they can be found in disproportionately large numbers in theologically conservative and evangelical seminaries. Second, they also can be found in disproportionately large numbers in churches in which the authority for credentialing and ordination is vested in the congregation, not in a denominational system.

Where Are the Megachurches?

One of the most publicized and widely discussed trends in American Protestantism during the past two decades has been the emergence of hundreds of very large congregations that average more than 800 at worship. In several denominations, somewhere between 1 and 2 percent of all congregations average more than 800 at worship. The Lutheran Church-Missouri Synod, the Southern Baptist Convention, the Baptist General Conference, the Episcopal Church, The Evangelical Free Church, the Presbyterian Church in America, and the Assemblies of God are examples of that pattern.

In most of the other mainline denominations, however, the proportion of megachurches is much lower. Less than one-sixth of 1 percent of all United Methodist congregations average more than 800 at worship. In the Presbyterian Church (U.S.A.) that proportion is less than one-half of 1 percent, and in the United Church of Christ it is one-ninth of 1 percent.

In most of the very large Protestant congregations in the United States that average more than 1,500 at worship, the authority for ordination rests in that worshiping community.

Where Do Blacks Worship?

A fourth trend may be the most highly visible. The vast majority of African Americans in church on Sunday morning can be found in churches in which the authority for ordination is placed in the congregation, not in a denominational board or committee.

While these four trends cannot be used to prove a cause-and-effect relationship, they do raise two interesting questions.

First, why are more and more Protestant churchgoers choosing churches in which the authority for ordination is vested in the congregation?

One part of the explanation can be found in a broad societal trend. Increasingly, North Americans are deserting hierarchical systems that call for decisions to be made in one place while the consequences of those decisions will be felt by people in another place. People are demanding greater control over the decisions that affect them personally. The Roman Catholic Church and The United Methodist Church are the two most highly visible victims of this trend in American Christianity.

What Are the Criteria?

Another part of the explanation lies in the differences in the choice of criteria. When the authority for ordination rests in a denominational board or committee, two factors often carry great weight. One is paper credentials. Has this candidate for ordination graduated with decent grades from a theological seminary that is acceptable to us? In some traditions, this is followed by a written examination. Thus the candidate who excels in academic skills is likely to be ordained.

In many traditions the second skill that is given considerable weight is competence in oral interviews. The articulate, quick-thinking, and personable candidate who can pass this "beauty contest" probably will be ordained.

By contrast, congregational leaders place a far higher value on three other criteria. One is character.[1] The person of good character (a) is concerned about the rights, feelings, and needs of others; (b) lives up to both oral and written commitments or promises; (c) accepts responsibility for the future consequences of present actions; (d) avoids deliberately threatening or harming others; and (e) respects other persons and the property rights of others.

It is difficult to test for character with a written test or by an oral interview. The most reliable method for evaluating character is to live with someone in times of tremendous stress, temptation, and pressure.

Congregational leaders also place a high value on Christian commitment. This also is easier to ascertain from life experiences than from academic exercises or oral interviews.

The third criterion that congregational leaders value is competence in ministry (see chap. 5). This also is easier to measure by performance than by tests or interviews.

What Are the Implications?

It will be far easier in the year 2033 than it is today to identify all the consequences of these emerging trends. Eight generalizations, however, can be offered with a reasonable degree of confidence.

The most obvious is that the churches that rank character, commitment, and competence above credentials probably will continue to attract a disproportionately large number of the churchgoers born after 1945.

The second is that those predominantly Anglo denominations that place the authority for ordination in the congregation probably will continue to have greater success in reaching African Americans than will those that place the authority in a denominational board or committee.

The third is that the very large multiple staff churches will come largely from among those congregations that attract, train, socialize, examine, and credential their future program staff from among their own members.

Overlapping that is a fourth generalization that is in conflict with tradition or church law in several denominations. Who will be the successor to the long-tenured senior minister of that large church? One alternative has been to seek someone with impressive academic credentials and a reputation as a scholar, executive, author, or senior pastor of another large congregation. An alternative has been to search for a bright, young, promising pastor in a smaller congregation who is ready to "move up" to a more challenging assignment. It often helped if that impressive young candidate had earned a degree from one of the prestigious theological seminaries of the 1950s, such as Princeton, Union of New York, Yale, Harvard, Chicago, Vanderbilt, Union of Richmond, Boston, or Concordia, St. Louis.

Today the best chances for a successful transition are with a successor who has served on the staff of that large congregation for several years, knows the distinctive culture of that church, has been able to earn the trust of the members, understands and is in sympathy with the priorities of the leaders, has been able to demonstrate a high level of professional competence in that local context, and is clearly perceived as a person of high moral character. It may help to have graduated from one of today's most widely respected theological seminaries (Princeton, Union of Richmond, and Concordia of St. Louis also would be on today's list of widely respected seminaries), but that would be far less of an asset than character, Christian commitment, and competence. If this is a very large congregation, there is one chance in five that the successor has never earned a degree from any theological seminary—and no one sees that as a liability.

The fifth implication, which is already clearly visible, is that megachurches are beginning to replace theological seminaries as the primary source for other large congregations seeking either lay or ordained program staff. Competence, Christian commitment, character, and understanding the distinctive culture of the megachurch are more valuable qualifications than academic credentials.

The sixth implication is a product of the first five. Those traditions that express the highest level of trust of the people are the ones most likely to attract the generations born after World War II. One expression of trust is in placing the authority for ordination in the congregation and trusting the people to choose the appropriate criteria for ordination.

Perhaps the greatest degree of unhappiness over this conflict in criteria is expressed by those who place a high value on academic preparation for the ministry and also hold serious misgivings about entrepreneurial gifts. This six-year-old new mission is served by a thirty-eight-year-old seminary graduate who also holds a Doctor of Ministry degree. Two years ago the congregation peaked in size with an average worship attendance of seventy, but three key families have moved recently, and that average is now down to sixty. Less than a mile away the five-year-old congregation founded by a Bible college graduate, who is now twenty-eight years old, averages close to six hundred at worship. Does this suggest the ecclesiastical marketplace values entrepreneurial gifts and competence more highly than academic preparation?

Finally, why are so many people who are approved for ordination by a denominational board or committee leaving the pastoral ministry after their first or second pastorate? Could it be that academic credentials are not as valuable or relevant as character, commitment, and competence?

13.

From Farm Clubs to Free Agents

What was the biggest change in theological education during the last half of the twentieth century? The answer will depend on the experiences and perspective of the person who responds. One admissions director replied, "The increasing number of students who are overwhelmed with credit card problems." A professor of New Testament answered, "Twenty years ago I spent most of the day either teaching or preparing to teach. Now I spend more time counseling students than I do in teaching, and I was trained to be a teacher, not a counselor." A seminary dean pointed out, "When I joined the faculty here, we had only three women in the Master of Divinity program. Today women account for nearly one-half of our M.Div. candidates."

The president of another seminary explained, "Thirty years ago our second-career students were drawn largely from men who gave up a promising future to enter the ministry. Today most of our second-career students—and we have a lot more of them than we had thirty years ago—are either women who have failed in marriage or men who have failed in business."

A newly retired denominational official who has been involved in ministerial placement since 1968 reflected, "The most significant change I have seen is not the increasing number of women or second-career students in seminary, it is the drop in quality. When I went to seminary, a fourth of my entering class had earned a Phi Beta Kappa key. Today it is rare to find a seminary student who was Phi Beta Kappa in college."

Another denominational executive did not hesitate when asked this question. "The big difference is debt. Every year I now interview new graduates who have accumulated $25,000 to $40,000 in debt. Right after they graduate, they have to begin making monthly payments of $200 to $600 on their debt. The other day I interviewed a forty-one-year-old graduate with a wife and three kids, two of whom are teenagers. He is looking forward to monthly payments of $400 on his debts plus $375 payments on a car loan. The only thing I could suggest was an interview with a small church that pays a cash salary of $19,000 plus a house, health insurance, utilities, and pension payments. They really can't afford that much. That whole compensation package takes nearly 60 percent of their total budget. He replied that he needed a cash salary of at least $26,000 plus benefits in order to be able to meet his obligations on his debts."

Another professor replied, "The most highly visible difference is the number of openly gay and lesbian students we now have. In retrospect, I realize that we always have had homosexuals in the ministry, but no one ever talked out loud in polite company about his or her sexual orientation."

A semi-retired pastor who was spending the last few years of his ministerial career teaching in a one-hundred-fifty-year-old seminary summarized his answer with these words: "Today's seminaries are faced with four competing sets of expectations. One group insists the seminary become a school of ideology. Another wants it to become a therapeutic center. A third believes it should be a school of theology. A fourth is convinced the focus should be on research—but that group is split between those who prefer the traditional library-centered academic research and those who want the research to focus on the context for parish ministry. What makes it worse is the faculty also is divided among those four sets of expectations."

"Unquestionably, the biggest difference since I entered seminary as a twenty-two-year-old in 1956 is the increased diversity in the student body," reflected another seminary professor. "In 1956 seminaries were filled with young white males. Today we have a far more diverse population with many more international students, a lot more women, many more older second-career students, a fair sprinkling of African Americans, Asian Americans, and Hispanics, and relatively few young white males. I'm a strong proponent of diversity, and I'm delighted to see this rich mosaic in both the student body and the faculty."

"You've raised the question that troubles our faculty the most," replied the dean of a large seminary. "For most of our history, this seminary took two assumptions for granted. The first was that every new student was a committed Christian. We on the faculty saw big differences among the incoming students in theological perspective and in their spiritual maturity, but close to 98 percent were clearly deeply committed Christians. Most of the exceptions were the sons of preachers who came to seminary because of parental pressures. The second assumption was that almost all of our incoming students were firmly committed to full-time service in the Christian ministry. Some planned to become missionaries, a few hoped for a career in teaching or as campus ministers, and nearly all the women who came expected to be either missionaries or directors of Christian education. Most of the men, however, were fully committed to becoming parish pastors. Repeatedly students told the faculty, 'All we want are the tools we need to be effective pastors.' Our primary role as a seminary was to prepare students to become pastors."

"How has that changed?" interrupted the visitor.

"Radically!" exclaimed the dean. "The most obvious evidence of this is we, like dozens of other seminaries, have had to create a new sequence we call Spiritual Formation. This is a required one-year sequence for all first-year students. It is designed to help those who are in the early stages of a spiritual pilgrimage deepen and strengthen their faith. In somewhat simplistic terms, it is a response to our reluctant recognition that many of our incoming students enroll in seminary, not to prepare for a career in ministry, but rather as part of their personal faith journey. They come to seminary, not to learn how to be pastors, but rather to learn how to strengthen their faith."

"The dean is putting the best possible face on this," interrupted another professor who was a part of that conversation. "We also have a fair number who come here to decide whether or not they want to be Christians. Others come to test their call to ministry. One evidence of that is less than one-half of our M.Div. graduates of twelve years ago are now in the parish ministry. Seminary today has become a place to test out your faith or to reflect on your call, rather than as a place to prepare oneself for doing parish ministry!"

"The easiest way to describe the differences is to look at the payroll," explained a professor in a small Midwestern seminary. "When I graduated from here in 1959, the number of students in the B.D. program was about the same as it is today for the M.Div. program, but we now have twice as many people on the payroll. We have five more professors, partly because we have added the D.Min. program and a couple of other degree programs. We also offer night and weekend classes for students with full-time jobs. When I was in school here, a student was not permitted to hold a full-time secular job. The administrative staff has tripled in number, and we now have two full-time people out recruiting new students. The student counseling center did not exist in 1959. Now it employs a full-time secretary and two full-time counselors plus a full-time person who oversees student loans and grants and offers counseling on financial problems. In 1959 this school offered two degree programs— the B.D. and the M.R.E. Now we offer six. We also have a full-time professor in field education and a full-time administrator overseeing the intern program. Neither of those positions existed in 1959. If you want to see how any organization has changed, begin by looking at the payroll!"[1]

What Is the Central Issue?

While this is far from a comprehensive list of the varied comments elicited by that opening question, they are sufficient to illustrate a point. One interpretation of these comments could be that today's theological seminaries are confronted with an unprecedented array of problems. That may be true. The ecclesiastical world of 1993 was far more complex than the world of 1953.

From my perspective, however, these and similar comments are largely a reflection of the two more basic issues. The first of these is the changing sources of students for theological seminaries.

A useful analogy is to look briefly at what has happened in major league baseball. Where does a major league baseball team turn to find the next generation of players? One answer was for the rich owner to purchase the contracts of stars from poorer owners. A more creative answer was devised by Branch Rickey of the St. Louis Cardinals in the 1920s when he designed an extensive system of minor league teams that recruited and trained amateur players. The major league team could depend on this system of "farm clubs" to produce the replacements when needed. This concept was copied by the New York Yankees in the 1930s and produced a long series of championship teams for that club.

The next big break in that tradition came in 1965 with the adoption of a draft of amateur players. Instead of the rich clubs monopolizing the talent, the draft helped to balance resources. Eleven years later the players won the right to become free agents after six years.

The result is that instead of depending solely on the talent developed on its farm clubs, today most major league teams look to the amateur draft and the occasional signing of a free agent to build a winning team.

For the first six or seven decades of the twentieth century, the denominationally affiliated theological seminaries also depended on their "farm clubs" for the next year's class of first-year students. These farm clubs included Sunday school teachers who told promising young men, "I believe God wants you to be a minister"; pastors who were happy and fulfilled in that vocation, modeled that role, and encouraged deeply committed young men to consider that calling; that "mountaintop" experience at the last night of summer church camp for high school students; campus ministers who encouraged promising students to go into the parish ministry; missionaries on furlough who stayed in the homes of devout church members and thus became inspiring models for the children in that home; church-related colleges that reinforced a culture that placed undergraduates planning to go to seminary at the top of the student deference pyramid; public school teachers who also were committed Christians and encouraged the call to the ministry by students who came to them to discuss that possibility; revivals that not only warmed the heart but also called for a vocational commitment; congregational leaders who automatically honored every young man when he announced his decision to enter the ministry; denominational systems that placed the enlistment of the next generation of ministers at or near the top of that institution's list of priorities; the public media that placed "men of the cloth" on a pedestal; parents who encouraged the cultural value that ideally their oldest son would become a minister; those congregations that boasted about the number of "Timothys" who had come out of that church; and the inspirational articles in the denominational magazines and Sunday school quarterlies.

In several denominations, that network of farm clubs has shrunk dramatically.

One successor consisted of the parachurch organizations that focused their efforts on high school, college, and university campuses. These organizations "graduated" large numbers of young people who have gone on to seminary—but most have chosen an evangelical and/or "transdenominational" school rather than a denominationally affiliated seminary. That source of seminary students also apparently peaked with the generation born in the 1956–68 era.

One result is that theological seminaries have, like major league baseball teams, turned to the amateurs and the free agents for the next generation of students to fill those classrooms. This usually means hiring a staff of scouts and recruiters. In baseball it means a financial bonus for signing. In higher education that bonus for signing up usually is called a "scholarship" or "student aid" or "free tuition."

The baseball scout hopes to recruit a slick fielding shortstop who can hit .300 or a lefthanded fastballer who can win twenty games, but the vast majority of players signed by the best scouts never play as many as a hundred games in the major leagues. How many star preachers and future transformational parish pastors should the admissions counselors on a seminary staff be expected to recruit? One a month? One a year? One every decade?

Perhaps the time has come to ask the hard question: Is it reasonable to expect that the free agents and amateurs can provide the parish pastors required for the twenty-first century? That long series of comments used to open this chapter suggests that not everyone is convinced the answer to that question is a resounding "Yes!"

That Second Issue

The second of the basic issues raised by those opening comments moves the discussion to a different question. Instead of examining the changing sources of seminary students, it may be more useful to ask where the next generation of parish pastors will come from in the twenty-first century.

Instead of turning to a baseball analogy, it may be instructive to turn to dairy farming. Ask the dairy farmer, "Where will your next generation of dairy cows come from?" The answer probably will be, "From the artificial insemination of my best cows with the semen of a top-quality bull."

Where should we seek to find the best parish pastors for the twenty-first century? Probably from within our best congregations that are led by our best pastors.

That already is happening. A growing number of self-identified teaching churches are accepting the responsibility for identifying, enlisting, training, screening, and credentialing a new generation of parish pastors. Before looking at that possibility in more detail, however, it is necessary to chase another rabbit briefly.

What is the best environment for the socialization of the next generation of parish pastors into that contemporary institutional expression of Christianity we call a worshiping community? The small rural church? Probably not, when one-half of today's churchgoers can be found in one-seventh of the churches. The church-related college campus? The very large and anonymous state university? The workplace? The home? The business world? The typical long-established Protestant congregation, which is gradually growing smaller in numbers as the members grow older? The seminary campus? Government employment? The military services? (During the 1975–94 era, this has produced a remarkable number of retirees who have gone into the parish ministry.)

Perhaps the best environment to socialize the next generation of parish pastors consists of those congregations that meet at least six or seven of the following nine criteria. These congregations (1) are unusually effective in reaching and serving the generations born after 1955 (these are the folks who will fill the pews in the churches in the year 2035 when few of us born before 1955 will be in church every Sunday morning); (2) most important of all, qualify as "transformational churches" in which people's lives are transformed by the power of the Gospel[2]; (3) can mobilize the resources necessary to place institutional survival goals on a secondary agenda while ministry goals dominate the primary agenda; (4) are able to offer people a range of choices in worship, music, the teaching ministry, opportunities for volunteer involvement in ministry in community outreach and mission beyond that community, personal and spiritual growth, and in other ministries; (5) enjoy the leadership of a long-tenured pastor or senior minister who is happy and fulfilled in the parish ministry, thus serving as an attractive model for future ministers; (6) possess the discretionary resources required to function as a teaching church without cutting back on that congregation's own ministry and outreach; (7) are located on the high-commitment end of the spectrum so they model the fact that effective ministry does require a high level of commitment; (8) include at least three or four volunteer leaders who enthusiastically support the concept that this congregation should be helping to enlist and train the generation of pastors needed for the twenty-first century; and (9) are able to place Christian commitment, character, and competence ahead of academic credentials and interviews in evaluating candidates for ordination. (See chap. 12.)

Your Place or Mine?

Before looking at alternative scenarios, the reader should not assume that the twenty-first century will bring the closing of theological seminaries. That is unlikely! Financial pressures will force the closing or merging of a few dozen, but most are too well-endowed and/or have the institutional strength to resist suggestions they close. Most will be able to attract students for incoming classes year after year and/or function as research centers and/or train people to serve for a decade, more or less, as pastors of smaller congregations and/or prepare people who seek employment in secular occupations and/or serve as centers for continuing adult education.

Where will the people in these churches secure the academic preparation that is required by several traditions for ordination? The answer to that question, of course, should model the value of choices.

A common pattern today is that person who commutes to seminary classrooms for the required academic courses while continuing to serve either as a volunteer or as a paid member of the program staff of that teaching church. A second option is for that future pastor to take a once-a-year three- or four-month leave of absence to be a full-time student on a seminary campus. A third is for that teaching church to have a resident faculty who teach all academic courses in classrooms in the teaching church's buildings. (Currently this is more common in the Southwest and West than elsewhere.) A growing alternative is for professors from an accredited seminary to come as visiting faculty and teach on that campus.

The most promising alternative is advocated by those who believe that television is here to stay. In 1984 a consortium of engineering schools and the National Technical University began telecasting, via satellite, lectures to offices, universities, and corporate offices. By 1992, the consortium had grown to forty-five schools including Cornell, Purdue, and the University of California at Berkeley.

The Public Broadcasting System (PBS) offers for-credit courses. In 1992 those programs enrolled 300,000 tuition-paying students, up from 55,000 a decade earlier.

One fringe benefit of distance learning, as this system is often called, is lower costs. A four-year degree program costs about one-fourth to one-third that required for a residential program.

Which seminaries will utilize current technology to aggressively develop cooperative arrangements with that growing number of teaching churches? At one time, some objectors argued this could not work because the teaching churches could not provide the library resources required for a degree program. That objection is now being made obsolete by the electronic storage of printed resources and electronic books. These and similar objections will continue to be diversionary issues.

The big issue is one of institutional turf and control. For decades the churches served as farm clubs sending students to seminaries. The teaching church concept reverses that relationship. Which theological seminaries will be willing to send (a) professors to help staff the classrooms in the teaching churches and/or (b) offer lectures via satellite to the teaching churches? Will the seminaries be willing to become farm clubs of the teaching churches? Some will contend that the answer can be found in Matthew 18:20. If two or three theological seminaries agree to accept a servant relationship to several dozen teaching churches, it matters little what the other 98 percent decide to do. An easy alternative would be for these teaching churches to sign up a faculty of free agents (retired professors, parish pastors with an earned doctorate from a research university who would like to teach part-time while continuing in the pastorate, etc.) who would teach the required academic courses.

The big issue, of course, should not be turf or control or accreditation, but rather which institutions will be most effective in recruiting the best and the brightest from among the babies born in the last quarter of the twentieth century and in socializing them into contemporary congregational life and ministry. Deciding which institutions can best provide the necessary academic preparation for the parish ministry is a secondary issue.

Which is the more promising place to look for the next generation of parish pastors: the teaching churches or theological seminaries? Who is better prepared to fulfill the mandate of Ephesians 4:12 in the twenty-first century?

14.

THE CHANGING ROLE OF DENOMINATIONS

A persuasive argument can be made that the larger Protestant denominations in the United States that came into existence before the Civil War reached their peak of influence during the 1950s. Their power, influence, internal loyalty, cohesion, and acceptance were greater during the 1950s than at any time before or since.[1]

One consequence of that is the denominational leaders who were ordained during the 1950s, and perhaps even into the early 1960s, see the 1950s role of denominations as normative. A second consequence is that most of those who refer to the 1950s as the normative benchmark for the role of denominations will have died or retired before the arrival of the third millennium.

During the past third of a century, however, the influence, authority, internal loyalty, and institutional strength of at least a dozen large Protestant denominations have been undermined by a series of events and trends. That list includes (1) schisms; (2) denominational mergers; (3) the popular support for greater interdenominational cooperation in the 1940s and the 1950s and the ecumenical movement of the 1960s; (4) the widening disapproval of anti-Catholicism, anti-Semitism, and racism as organizing principles to reinforce a group identity against a common enemy; (5) affluence; (6) the competition of a growing number of parachurch organizations and affinity groups created to service congregations, pastors, and volunteer leaders; (7) the emergence of scores of very large congregations in which the leaders are convinced "the denomination needs us more than we need them"; (8) the emergence of new nondenominational agencies that enlist, screen, train, place, and support missionaries; (9) technological advances such as the computer and desktop publishing; (10) the replacement of the printed word by visual communication as the most powerful channel of communication with the general public; (11) the general erosion of institutional loyalties in American society; (12) the high priority given to highly divisive social justice issues by the national conventions of several denominations; (13) the emergence and high visibility of scores of teaching churches that either do not carry a denominational identity or carry it very lightly and service other congregations; (14) the general drift of denominational agencies toward a more liberal theological position while younger generations of churchgoers tend to be oriented toward an evangelical stance; (15) the sharp decrease in the number of congregational leaders, both lay and ordained, who appreciate having people in distant offices make decisions that will affect that congregation; (16) the preference of an increasing number of large financial contributors for opportunities for designated second-mile giving over contributing to a unified budget; (17) the growing proportion of candidates for the ministry who choose not to enroll in a theological seminary of their denomination; (18) the gradual elimination of regionalism as a significant source of any institution's distinctive identity; (19) the growing number of interdenominational and interfaith marriages; (20) the reduction in denominational resources allocated to world missions and new church development—two of the causes that earlier had aroused strong support from both the laity and the clergy as well as justification for the existence of denominational agencies; (21) the creation of local, regional, and national coalitions across denominational lines by the senior ministers of very large congregations; (22) in response to the admonitions from denominational leaders "to serve your community" and "to find mission in your own backyard," thousands of congregations have done that—and one result is their ties to their community are now stronger than the ties to their denomination, the reverse of the typical 1955 pattern; (23) the emerging adversarial relationships between many denominational agencies and congregational leaders has replaced the old lay-clergy division[2]; (24) the divisions within denominational leadership over separation of church and state issues, such as government financed vouchers for children attending private schools, the tax exemption of religious property, governmental subsidies for church-owned and operated private housing, and governmental grants to students attending church-owned and operated colleges and theological seminaries; (25) a serious breakdown in the consensus of the 1950s on what are the appropriate and necessary roles and responsibilities of denominations; (26) the financial squeeze felt by many national denominational agencies in the late 1980s and the early 1990s; and (27) perhaps most significant of all in the long term, the decision by a growing number of pastors and volunteer leaders to invest their time, energy, creativity, and money in new local interchurch coalitions they have helped to create, rather than in inherited institutional structures in which they feel they do not have a meaningful voice.

What Are the Implications?

During the second half of the twentieth century, two exceptionally influential patterns of institutional behavior could be observed in American Protestantism. The more highly visible, and to some the more lamentable, was the erosion of the power and influence of denominational agencies and leaders described here.

One product of this has been the weakening of the role of interdenominational agencies that draw the policy making members of their governing boards and/or their financial resources largely from denominational systems. A parallel is the trade association composed of owners of drive-in theaters that flourished back in the 1950s when the countryside was covered with thousands of outdoor movie screens. The multi-screen cineplexes in or near the shopping malls, the popularity of the VCR, and the easy availability of videotapes have wiped out most of the clientele for the drive-in theater. One result has been a shrinking of dollar receipts. A second has been the loss of thousands of jobs.

The second of these two highly significant trends has been both a cause and a product of the first. This has been the creation of dozens of new single-purpose networks. Rather than create the elaborate institutional apparatus required for a denominational structure, the focus of these networks has been on mission and ministry.

The contrast between these two trends is symbolized by two organizations. The older of the two is the Consultation on Church Union (COCU), created in 1962 to encourage the merger of four large denominations plus any other interested bodies. The stated goal was to create a new denomination that would be "truly catholic and truly reformed." As the years passed, several other denominations joined this consultation.

The newer of the two officially came into existence in 1991. This is Churches Uniting in Global Mission (CUGM). Its origins go back to October 1990, when ten senior pastors from a broad variety of traditions came together. They prayed about how they and their congregations might address the most pressing spiritual, social, and missional issues of this era. This movement's number-one concern is "to bear witness to a secular, sinful, and suffering world of the healing and hopeful gospel of Jesus Christ."

This new coalition includes senior pastors from several oldline denominations, including United Methodist, Presbyterian, Lutheran, Episcopal, Southern Baptist, United Church of Christ, Reformed, and American Baptist as well as independent, charismatic, Holiness, Christian, Assemblies of God, and other traditions.

Five differences between these two movements illustrate the emergence of a new era in interchurch cooperation.

1. COCU was created to advance institutional mergers. CUGM was created to advance mission, witness, and outreach.
2. The leadership of COCU is vested largely in denominational structures and denominational officers. The leadership of CUGM is vested in senior ministers.
3. COCU brings together people from a relatively narrow band of Protestant traditions. CUGM brings leaders together from a huge array of traditions from liberal to fundamentalist.
4. After many years of frustration in promoting organic union, COCU has moved cooperation in ministry to the top of the agenda. Within weeks of its official birth, CUGM had delivered tons of food to hungry people in Russia.
5. COCU works with and through denominational structures. CUGM works with and through individuals, congregations, and ad hoc groups.

From the perspective of the twenty-first century, perhaps the central point in this chapter is the shift in identification of the partners for interchurch cooperation. In the first five or six decades of the twentieth century, the initiators and the key players were denominations and denominational officials. During the last two decades of the century, that has shifted to pastors and congregational leaders with an especially highly visible role for the senior pastors of large congregations.

Churches Uniting in Global Mission is only one of several of the new networks. The Leadership Network, headquartered in Tyler, Texas, came into existence in the early 1980s to assist senior pastors of large churches.

The Willow Creek Association was created in 1990 to provide a variety of resources for congregations seeking to minister to the unchurched.

These are but three of dozens of coalitions, networks, movements, and associations that have emerged in the closing years of the twentieth century. They came into existence in response to the needs of pastors and congregational leaders. These needs were not being met by the traditional structures of American Protestantism, such as denominations, theological seminaries, church-related colleges, councils of churches, and older parachurch organizations. Instead of seeking to reform the old, these impatient congregational leaders concluded it would be easier, faster, and more effective to create new structures.[3]

One product of this impatience has been the creation of a rapidly growing number of teaching churches. More and more of the continuing education experiences for ministers, professional staff members, and volunteer leaders that once were offered by denominational agencies, colleges, seminaries, councils of churches, and parachurch organizations are now designed and offered by individual congregations. Of special significance is the capability and willingness of several of these large teaching churches "to take the show on the road" and offer continuing education events in various parts of the world.

A second product of this impatience is the planting of new missions. Back in the 1950s and 1960s, this need was met largely by denominations. In recent years a growing proportion of all new missions are the creation of either one congregation or a coalition of churches.

A third, and one of the older products of this impatience, is the growing number of organizations and networks that recruit, screen, place, and support missionaries. What was a near monopoly for denominations back in the 1950s is now a remarkable example of personal initiative, creativity, congregational cooperation, pluralism, and independence.

One of the more interesting products of this impatience with reforming the old can be seen in a huge variety of social welfare and social justice ministries organized by congregational leaders around God's grace. By contrast, many denominational agencies prefer a legalistic approach to social welfare and social justice issues.

A fifth product of this impatience is the rapidly growing number of ad hoc movements designed to create and distribute videotapes and other teaching resources as well as new hymns and choruses and other aids for worship and drama.

What Is the Future of Your Denomination?

The erosion of the traditional roles, power, and functions of denominational systems plus the effectiveness of these new coalitions, networks, and ad hoc groups has caused more and more leaders to raise serious questions about the future of denominations. What will be the role of denominational structures in the twenty-first century?

One widely publicized response has been to identify denominations as "cultural dinosaurs." This term allegedly was coined by Professor Robert Wuthnow, but perhaps the most realistic appraisal has been offered by Craig Dykstra and James Hudnut-Beumler. As they trace the evolutionary history of denominational structures in American Protestantism, they conclude that the corporate bureaucratic structure created in the nineteenth century began to break down in the 1960s. They identify the regulatory agency model as the successor to the denomination once organized around mission, credentialing the clergy, and resourcing congregations.[4]

This new role is most visible in connectional denominations such as The United Methodist Church, the Presbyterian Church (U.S.A.), the Episcopal Church and, to a lesser degree, the new Evangelical Lutheran Church in America. It is more difficult for those denominations with a congregational polity to seek to function as a regulatory agency. Despite the limitations of polity, leaders in several congregational-type polity denominations have sought to adopt this role. Examples include the Lutheran Church-Missouri Synod, the Southern Baptist Convention, the United Church of Christ, and the Christian Reformed Church.

How does a denomination function as a regulatory agency?

It adopts rules and regulations that must be followed by individuals, congregations, and regional judicatories as well as by national agencies. Examples include the credentials required for ordination (see chap. 12); procedures for removing a member's name from a congregational membership roster; permission to relocate a congregation's meeting place; a requirement that race, gender, age, color, nationality, or marital status cannot be considered as factors in filling a vacant pulpit; quotas for selecting delegates to regional and national conventions and to denominational boards; the adoption of a minimum salary for pastors; minimum standards for congregational contributions to the denominational treasury; mandatory retirement at a specified age; requirements for continuing education for pastors; restrictions on designated second-mile giving by contributors; regulations on marriage, divorce, remarriage, sexual orientation, abortion, and cohabitation; restrictions on who will be admitted to the table for the Lord's Supper; restrictions on involvement in interchurch activities; and criteria for selection of volunteers to serve on committees and boards.

The Price Tag on That New Role

Everything in this life, except grace, carries a price tag. This new role of denominations as regulatory agencies is not an exception to that generalization. One price tag is increased internal conflict and division. One reason for that is the number of people who enjoy the role of regulating the belief patterns and behavior of others is far larger than the number who appreciate having someone else regulate their beliefs and behavior. A second reason is that most regulations are divisive.

The divisive nature of denominational regulations was illustrated most clearly in the summer of 1992. The policy making board of the American Baptist Churches in the U. S. A. rejected—by a vote of 91 to 8—a resolution condemning homosexuality.

The all-male delegates to the Synod 1992 Convention of the Christian Reformed Church voted by a 109-73 margin to continue to prohibit the ordination of women, although women constitute a majority of the adult members of that denomination.

The Lutheran Church-Missouri Synod voted 66 to 44 to adopt a new regulatory system for resolving conflict. It also elected—by a 580 to 568 margin—a new Synod president who appeared to favor a stronger regulatory role for that denomination's central agencies.

Potentially one of the most crucial decisions by a national denomination to accept the role of a regulatory agency came at the May 1992 General Conference of The United Methodist Church. By a vote of 512 to 421, the delegates mandated participation by every annual conference in a proposed denomination-wide health care program for ministers and other church employees. Many saw this as a radical change that reduced the authority of the annual conferences and greatly expanded the authority of the national church. The action of the General Conference was appealed by several annual conferences to the Judicial Council, which is the equivalent of the Supreme Court for The United Methodist Church. In late 1992 the Judicial Council overruled the action of the General Conference.

In the fall of 1992 the Permanent Judicial Commission of the Presbyterian Church (U.S.A.) overruled earlier actions by a synod and presbytery in approving the call of Jane Spahr to the staff of the Downtown United Presbyterian Church in Rochester, New York.

A reasonable projection, based on history, is that as the regulatory authority of the denominations increases, the number of congregations voting to secede will increase. An alternative scenario is that an increase in the role of the denomination as a regulatory agency will coincide with greater difficulty in reaching adults born after 1945.

The perception that denominations have evolved from organizations designed to resource congregations into regulatory agencies is one reason offered by both younger clergy and younger laypersons to explain their membership in an independent or nondenominational congregation.

The most significant implication of this new role of denominations as regulatory agencies centers on one simple word: *trust*. The obvious implication of this growing emphasis on regulation by distant denominational agencies is that the volunteer leaders and the ministers in the local situation cannot be trusted. The consequences of that stance for the twenty-first century should be obvious to anyone who is well acquainted with (a) the college educated lay leaders in today's congregations, (b) African-Americans, (c) immigrants from the Pacific Rim, (d) women born after 1930, (e) individual entrepreneurs who founded and operated a successful business, and (f) farmers.

From an institutional perspective, another implication is that this change in priorities by denominational agencies will increase the role of parachurch organizations, individual entrepreneurs, megachurches, theological seminaries, and retreat centers in resourcing congregations. They will continue to fill the vacuum created by this evolving role of denominations.

From a long-term perspective, a reasonable projection is the numerically growing denominations of the twenty-first century will be those that (a) place the resourcing of congregations, mobilizing resources for worldwide mission, the planting of new churches, encouraging the emergence of more large congregations, and enlisting a new generation of highly competent and deeply committed pastors as the top five priorities for that denomination and (b) display a high level of trust toward congregational leaders. Those that concentrate their resources on their regulatory role probably will shrink in numbers.

15.

THE BIGGEST CLOUD ON THE HORIZON

What will determine the shape of American Protestantism in the twenty-first century? Unquestionably the most influential single factor will be the quality, the commitment, the value, the traits, the goals, the character, the priorities, the competence, the productivity, and the theological stance of the next generation of parish pastors. The pastors in the year 2032 will be drawn largely from among the people born in the last third of the twentieth century. Which denominations will be able to attract into the parish ministry the best of the best and brightest of today's seventeen-year-olds and of tomorrow's babies? Many see the identification, enlistment, screening, education, and placement as the number-one responsibility of denominational systems. Thus in some traditions this variable is under the control of denominational leaders. If they fail, the backup system is congregations. If congregations play a larger role in fulfilling this responsibility, this may mean that denominations may be supplanted by networks or coalitions of large churches. That change, incidentally, is already well underway.[1]

In most of the numerically growing traditions, the primary responsibility for identifying and enlisting the next generation of pastors rests solely or largely on congregations.

Another variable will be the ability of American Protestantism to reach and minister with new generations of American-born adults and with the millions of immigrants who come to these shores every decade. Traditionally, the most effective means of accomplishing this has been through the organization of new congregations. The capability of long-established congregations to do this is limited by a series of natural institutional factors that tend to make care of today's members the top local priority. On the surface it appears this responsibility is in the hands of existing congregations and denominational leaders. Therefore, the future will be shaped in large part by today's leaders.

That, however, now appears to be an excessively simplistic view of contemporary reality. It now appears that the twenty-first century may resemble the second half of the twentieth century rather than the first half in one remarkably significant way. This is the legal restrictions on the use of land for religious purposes. Thus the views of the courts on the use of land move ahead of strategies for new church development as the second most crucial variable in shaping American Protestantism in the twenty-first century.

Up until 1949 it was almost universally assumed that churches were legally acceptable uses in any district zoned for residences. The first municipal zoning ordinance in the United States was adopted by New York City in 1916. Twenty years later, Edward M. Bassett, one of the principal authors of that ordinance, wrote a textbook on zoning. He commented that it never occurred to those who drafted that resolution "that there was the remotest possibility that churches, schools, and hospitals could properly be excluded from any districts."[2]

In 1949, however, the California Court of Appeals ruled that a zoning ordinance in Porterville that banned churches from an entire residential district was constitutionally valid. That decision was appealed by the plaintiff, a Mormon congregation, to both the California State Supreme Court and the United States Supreme Court. Both courts refused to review it.

During the next several decades the judicial precedents supporting those who oppose the use of land for religious purposes have become increasingly numerous.

One of the more widely cited recent precedents came when the City of Lakewood, Ohio, refused a building permit to a Jehovah's Witnesses congregation. The court held that the construction of a place of worship was a secular activity and, therefore, the refusal to grant a building permit did not impose a burden on the practice of religion. This decision was affirmed in 1983 in the United States Court of Appeals for the Sixth Circuit.[3]

More recently, and even more threatening, is the decision by the United States Supreme Court in 1990 in *Oregon Employment Division v. Smith*. In this case the court ruled that the government does not have to accommodate any "incidental" burdens on religion that result from the enforcement of a "reasonable law." This replaces the historic "compelling public interest" assumption that declared government must demonstrate a compelling public interest when interfering with constitutionally supported religious practices.

What this means is that municipal and county governments can restrict the use of land for religious uses. Why would they do that? In many cases because the neighbors (voters) object to construction of a church building on nearby property. In other cases, the local government wants that property to remain on the tax roll. In other situations, the leaders of a nearby congregation object to potential competition. Frequently the surface argument is about an increased volume of traffic or obstruction of a view or congestion of nonresidents using local streets or potential weeknight use or the presence of a large number of noisy children.

The most common scenario involves a congregation that purchases a parcel of land with the intent to construct a building on that site. When they seek zoning approval and/or a building permit, objections are raised. In some cases, permission is refused. In others, it is accompanied by so many restrictions that the proposed construction program is no longer feasible. The congregation's legal counsel advises, "If you go to court and are willing to appeal the initial decision if you lose, you have two chances out of three in winning. This may cost you three years' time and as much as a million dollars." The congregational leaders turn away sorrowfully and either agree to the restrictions or purchase another site. Thus another local precedent is established to justify increased restrictions on the use of land for religious uses. If and when the United States Supreme Court rules on this question, that ruling will become the second most influential factor in shaping religion in the United States in the twenty-first century.

Until that ruling is made, it is unlikely that local units of government will become more sympathetic to the use of land for religious purposes.

What Are the Alternatives?

One result of the present state of the case law is that literally hundreds of congregations have had to settle for what they believed was a second- or third-rate site in order to secure a building permit. In Colorado, one congregation was denied a building permit on a thirty-five acre site they had purchased in a residential district. After many months of frustration, they gave up and purchased a nearby new shopping mall at an 80 percent discount from the construction cost.

Many others have yielded and accepted the restrictions demanded by neighbors.

A growing number have decided to go the political route and support candidates for public office who promise to be supportive of the use of land for religious uses. (This represents a concession to the concept that rule by human beings is more realistic than relying on the rule of law.)

A few have spent the time and money required to win a favorable decision in a state appeals court.

A couple have purchased huge tracts, developed the periphery of the site with residential buildings and either sold or rented those residences to people who will be supportive of the development of the rest of that parcel for religious uses.

Several congregations have decided to remodel their present property when they could not secure the permits required for relocation.

Others have purchased or leased an existing structure in a commercial or industrial district when they were unable to secure a permit to build in a residential area.

What will the courts and/or the legislatures do to resolve this issue? At the moment this appears to be the biggest cloud on the ecclesiastical horizon as we prepare to enter the third millennium.

16.

TWENTY-ONE BRIDGES TO THE TWENTY-FIRST CENTURY

A Gallup poll in 1955 reported that only one adult in twenty-five had switched from the religious tradition in which he or she had been reared to another denomination or faith.

A similar poll in 1992 reported that six adults out of twenty-five had changed religious affiliation at least once since childhood.

What are the patterns in this accelerating religious migration? Perhaps the most significant is that regular worship attenders are more likely to switch than are less regular attenders. Intermarriage motivated one-fourth of the recent changes. The denominations losing the largest proportion of members from this migration reported in the early 1990s were Roman Catholics, Methodists, Southern Baptists, Lutherans, and Presbyterians.

What Is the Direction of the Flow?

In broad general terms this ecclesiastical migration can be described by picturing twenty-one bridges connecting two destinations. Traffic across each bridge consists of two streams, one going in each direction. Which are the larger streams across each bridge?

1. From low-expectation churches to high-commitment covenant communities.

2. From older congregations to newer churches.

3. From low-quality to high-quality ministries.

4. From congregations that concentrate most of their program on Sunday morning to those with a seven-day-a-week schedule.

5. From smaller to larger congregations.

6. From Roman Catholic parishes to Protestant churches. (In the 1950s the Protestant-to-Catholic migration was three times the size of the stream in the other direction. By 1990 these proportions had been reversed.)

7. From congregations composed largely of members born before 1940 to those with larger proportions of younger members.

8. From congregations with a limited teaching ministry to those with an extensive teaching ministry.

9. From churches that offer dull and boring worship services to those with exciting worship experiences.

10. From congregations with one chancel choir to those with two or three music groups in every worship service.

11. From those that rely exclusively on the organ and the piano for instrumental music to those with a band or orchestra or a more varied range of instrumental music.

12. From congregations that choose their hymns largely from those written before 1930 to churches that frequently choose hymns and choruses composed since 1980 as a part of their corporate worship.

13. From ecclesiastical systems that place control over major policy, program, and personnel concerns in external or distant places of authority to congregations that are completely self-governing. (This is a partial explanation for the Catholic-to-Protestant migration.)

14. From Jewish to Christian.

15. From churches with twelve- to twenty-minute sermons to those with longer sermons and longer worship services.

16. From congregations with little or no off-street parking to those with adequate off-street parking.

17. From those without air conditioning to those with air conditioning.

18. From those with a modest emphasis on missions to those that are organized around three central foci—(a) worship, (b) teaching, and (c) missions.

19. From non-charismatic congregations to charismatic churches.

20. From congregations with a series of short pastorates to those with long pastorates.

21. From congregations organized almost entirely around "doing good" and often neglecting the spiritual needs of their members, to churches that place at the top of the local priority list obedience to Jesus' threefold command, "Feed my sheep!" (see John 21:15-17).

The receiving congregations at the end of this stream place a high priority on responding to the religious needs of the self-identified seekers, searchers, inquirers, pilgrims, and others who are on a religious quest. The larger stream of people across this bridge are those going to the churches that conceptualize their ministry in a four-part sequence. The first is to respond in a meaningful way to those teenagers and adults who are on a quest for faith. Part two is built around a strong teaching ministry. Part three is challenging these sojourners to a commitment to discipleship. Part four, which overlaps the second and third stages, is sending people out to do ministry. (See chap. 10 for an expanded statement of this sequence.)

Two Other Streams

Two other smaller streams that overlap one or more of the larger streams described above also merit mention. One consists of people leaving churches that offer dull and boring worship services, that seek to induce a deeper sense of guilt in the people and are largely maintenance ministries that also largely neglect the call to social welfare and social justice ministries. This stream flows to those churches that have earned a reputation for neighbor-centered outreach ministries and missions.

A parallel small stream is from churches that fill the air with rhetoric about discipleship, but do nothing to help the pilgrims and sojourners become committed disciples. These pilgrims leave in search of a church that conceptualizes membership as a way station on the road to discipleship rather than as a destination or as a guaranteed ticket to heaven or as an obligation to support an institution.

Caution: Most of these migrations across a huge variety of ecclesiastical bridges are two-way streets! Some people do leave the high-commitment parish for a low-expectation congregation. Others do prefer the intimacy, spontaneity, and fellowship of the small church. Christians do convert to Judaism. Protestants do become Catholic. Many leave complexity in their search for simplicity. Thousands of second- or third-generation fundamentalists leave certainty for ambiguity. The traffic moves in both directions over every one of these bridges! The largest volume of traffic, as we approach the third millennium, is in the directions described earlier.

What Are the Implications?

These migration patterns confront both denominational and congregational policy makers with crucial questions as they look ahead to the twenty-first century. The obvious, number-one question is simple to articulate but difficult to answer. Do we go with the flow or do we go against the dominant migration trend? Often it is easier to go with the flow.

The two *big* exceptions to that last sentence are important for planning for a new day. One exception is that it usually is more attractive to seek to perpetuate the status quo. This may not be easy to accomplish, but it can attract strong support. In real life that often means going against the larger of those two streams of traffic across any one of those twenty-one bridges. For example, it often is easier for a congregation or denomination to grow older in terms of the age of the constituency and smaller in numbers than it is to reach and serve new generations of people with differing expectations of the church.

The second big exception overlaps the first. It is easier to go in the direction that requires minimal change. The most common example of this is the aging congregation that concentrates its efforts on reaching mature adults. A second is the congregation that is faced with the fact that reaching new generations means a seven-day-a-week program that is impossible in this building at this site. Rather than relocate, the decision is made to remain at this site and seek to raise the quality of the Sunday morning program.

A third example is the congregation that has always acted out the belief that worship is for adults and Sunday school is for women and children. That is reinforced by "the one-hour package" on Sunday morning with worship and Sunday school at the same hour. Rather than raise expectations by moving toward becoming a high-commitment church in which everyone is expected to be involved in *both* worship *and* Sunday school every week, the decision is made to raise the money to repair the aging pipe organ or to purchase new hymnals or to replace the roof or to remodel the kitchen and restrooms.

The most obvious implication is that the numerically growing congregations and denominations in the first years of the third millennium will be those that are both able and willing to make the changes necessary to respond in a meaningful way to the religious needs of skeptics, seekers, searchers, inquirers, and pilgrims who will be crossing these bridges in the years ahead.

NOTES

Introduction

1. A brilliant book on changes required for a new era in ministry by a remarkably effective parish pastor is Leith Anderson, *A Church for the 21st Century* (Minneapolis: Bethany House Publishers, 1992). An excellent book by a veteran religious journalist is Russell Chandler, *Racing Toward 2001* (Grand Rapids, Mich.: Zondervan Publishing House, 1992).

2. A provocative historical account of the decline of the mainline denominations and the emergence of a huge new array of evangelical churches is Roger Finke and Rodney Stark, *The Churching of America, 1776–1990* (New Brunswick, N.J.: Rutgers University Press, 1992).

3. A superb diagnostic and prescriptive statement on reaching new generations is George G. Hunter III, *How to Reach Secular People* (Nashville: Abingdon Press, 1992).

1. The Call to High Commitment

1. These two paragraphs are based on an article by Hilary Stout, "Remedial Curriculum for Low Achievers Is Falling from Favor," *The Wall Street Journal,* July 30, 1992, p. 1.

2. *The Connecticut Mutual Life Insurance Company Report on American Values in the '80s: The Impact of Belief* (Hartford: The Connecticut Mutual Life Insurance Company, 1981).

3. The emergence of a new group of high-commitment churches on the American scene who are growing in numbers while the low-

commitment mainline Protestant denominations shrink in size is a central theme of Roger Finke and Rodney Starke, *The Churching of America, 1776–1990* (New Brunswick, N.J.: Rutgers University Press, 1992).

4. For an excellent example of a call to reform a denomination, see Milton J. Coalter, John M. Mulder, and Louis B. Weeks, *The Reforming Tradition* (Louisville: Westminster/John Knox Press, 1992), pp. 245-87. The authors declare "reform begins with repentance" and go on to contend that "reform means recovery of a theological vision."

5. See Lyle E. Schaller, *Strategies for Change* (Nashville: Abingdon Press, 1993), chapter 7.

2. Rules to Relationships

1. William Glasser, *The Identity Society* (New York: Harper & Row, 1972).

3. The Most Startling Change

1. The concept of the teaching church is described in Lyle E. Schaller, *The Seven-Day-A-Week Church* (Nashville: Abingdon Press, 1992), pp. 29-32.

4. The Big Boxes Are Here!

1. The nationally publicized response of one small town to the arrival of a Wal-Mart store is described by Donald Dale Jackson, "It's Wake-Up Time for Main Street When Wal-Mart Comes to Town," *Smithsonian,* October 1992, pp. 36-47. That threat is discussed from the pharmacist's perspective by Tim Simmons, "Invincible?" *Supermarket News,* August 10, 1992, p. 2.

5. Performance Counts!

1. An excellent critique of interdenominational cooperation can be found in Roger Finke and Rodney Stark, *The Churching of America, 1776–1990* (New Brunswick, N.J.: Rutgers University Press, 1992).

6. Choices and Quality

1. One explanation for why congregational mergers rarely produce the hoped for results is found in Lyle E. Schaller, *Reflections of a Contrarian* (Nashville: Abingdon Press, 1989), pp. 136-49.

2. William Glasser, *The Quality School* (New York: HarperCollins, 1990).

7. A New Generation of Young Adults

1. Ed Janko, "A Tale of Two Yearbooks," *The College Board Review* (Spring 1992): 2-5. An earlier example of an adult comparing the high school of his youth with one a generation later is James Q. Wilson, *On Character* (Washington, D.C.: The AEI Press, 1991). In chapter 6, Wilson recalls his days at Jordan High School in North Long Beach, California. In chapter 7, this renowned scholar describes what he saw and heard in 1969, twenty-one years after his graduation.

2. For a longer discussion on generational theory, see Lyle E. Schaller, *Reflections of a Contrarian* (Nashville: Abingdon Press, 1989), pp. 65-95.

3. For a provocative discussion of the typographic era, see Neil Postman, *Amusing Ourselves to Death* (New York: Penguin Books, 1985), chapters 3 and 4.

4. A valuable resource for leaders interested in reaching these generations is George Barna, *The Invisible Generation: Baby Busters* (Glendale, Calif.: Barna Research Group, Ltd., 1992).

8. Where Are the Younger Males?

1. Dean Kelley, *Why Conservative Churches Are Growing* (San Francisco: Harper & Row, 1972).

2. Tucker Carlson, "That Old-Time Religion," *Policy Review* (Summer 1992): 13-17. A survey of 2,150 black congregations from the seven major historic black Protestant denominations reported male membership averaged 30 percent. See C. Eric Lincoln and Lawrence H. Mamiya, *The Black Church in the African American Experience* (Durham, N.C.: Duke University Press, 1990), p. 304. These two scholars suggest that American society has delegated "cultural main-

tenance and value transmission" to women and that is a partial explanation for the large proportion of women in churches.

3. An exceptionally good study on the migration of adults from Catholic and liberal Protestant congregations to a new evangelical tradition is Robin D. Perrin and Armand L. Mauss, "Saints and Seekers: Sources of Recruitment to the Vineyard Christian Fellowship," *Review of Religious Research* 33, 2 (December 1991).

9. Worshiping with New Generations

1. See "The Wrap on Cheese," *Supermarket News,* August 10, 1992, p. 44.

2. George Plagenz, "Pulpit Must Be Good Theater," *The Pueblo Chieftain,* August 20, 1988.

3. Robert Randall, *What People Expect From Church* (Nashville: Abingdon Press, 1993), chapter 5.

4. See Michael W. Harris, *The Rise of Gospel Blues* (New York: Oxford University Press, 1992).

5. Brent Bowers, "Hard Sell: Organs Make Pretty Music for Florida Mall Man," *Wall Street Journal,* October 1, 1992, p. 1.

12. Credentials or Character, Commitment, and Competence?

1. The growing concern about how a society nurtured people of good character is illustrated by two recent books. One is a collection of essays by James Q. Wilson, *On Character* (Washington, D.C.: The AEI Press, 1991). Wilson is a white male neoconservative who gained fame from his research and writing on crime and punishment. He finally concluded that the decay of human character is the major source of criminal behavior. The second book, Marian Wright Edelman, *The Measure of Our Success: A Letter to My Children and Yours* (Boston: Beacon Press, 1992), is by a liberal black woman who is a longtime close friend of Hillary Clinton. Both authors, however, emphasize the importance of building good character into the next generation of adults in this nation, and both underscore the same basic value system.

13. From Farm Clubs to Free Agents

1. The comments quoted here are drawn from conversations with faculty and administrators from three dozen theological seminaries and various denominational executives. A more incisive statement was offered by Professor Robert W. Jensen, "So Why Did Braaten Do It?" *Dialog* 30 (Autumn 1991): 262-63. A thoughtful statement by a seminary dean on one facet of this issue is Robin Lovin, "The Real Task of Practical Theology," *The Christian Century,* February 5-12, 1992, pp. 125-28. A provocative statement by a veteran of this debate is Loren B. Mead, "Seminary and Church: Missing Ministry," *The Christian Century,* April 26, 1989, pp. 450ff. The issue of financing higher education is discussed in a challenging essay by Thomas Sowell, "The Scandal of College Tuition," *Commentary* (August 1992): 23-26. In an earlier book, I deplored the excessive expectations placed on theological seminaries; see Lyle E. Schaller, "What Do You Expect of the Seminaries?" *Reflections of a Contrarian* (Nashville: Abingdon Press, 1989), pp. 171-83. A popular essay that aroused widespread attention when it was published is Paul Wilkes, "The Hands That Would Shape Our Souls," *The Atlantic,* December 1990, pp. 59-88.

2. These churches are described briefly in Lyle E. Schaller, *The Seven-Day-A-Week Church* (Nashville: Abingdon Press, 1992), p. 14.

14. The Changing Role of Denominations

1. A more detailed analysis of the decline of denominationalism can be found in Robert Wuthnow, *The Restructuring of American Religion* (Princeton, N.J.: Princeton University Press, 1988), chap. 5. See also Lyle E. Schaller, *The Seven-Day-A-Week Church* (Nashville: Abingdon Press, 1992), chap. 1. For an argument that a couple of denominations peaked in size and influence back in the nineteenth century, see Roger Finke and Rodney Stark, *The Churching of America, 1776–1990* (New Brunswick, N.J.: Rutgers University Press, 1992), pp. 145-72, 237-55.

2. Back in the 1960s, many observers of American Protestantism pointed to the differences in values, goals, and priorities between the laity and the clergy as the dark cloud on the horizon. By 1990 it had become clear that the crucial division was not between the laity and

the clergy, but rather between congregational leaders, both lay and clergy, and denominational officials. A superb summary from a Presbyterian perspective of the research on this issue plus a prescription for reform is Milton J. Coalter, John M. Mulder, and Louis B. Weeks, *The Re-Forming Tradition* (Louisville: Westminster/John Knox Press, 1992).

3. The temptation for contemporary leaders to create new coalitions rather than invest that time and energy in reforming old organizations is described in Lyle E. Schaller, *Strategies for Change* (Nashville: Abingdon Press, 1993), chap. 7.

4. Craig Dykstra and James Hudnut-Beumler, "The National Organizational Structures of Protestant Denominations: The Invitation to a Conversation," in *The Organizational Revolution,* edited by Milton J. Coalter, John M. Mulder, and Louis Weeks (Louisville: Westminster/John Knox Press, 1992), pp. 307-33.

15. The Biggest Cloud on the Horizon

1. See Lyle E. Schaller, *The Seven-Day-A-Week Church* (Nashville: Abingdon Press, 1992).

2. Edward Murray Bassett, *Zoning: The Laws, Administration, and Court Decisions During the First Twenty Years* (New York: Russell Sage Foundation, 1940).

3. The Lakewood, Ohio, case and related issues are discussed in more detail in Scott David Godshall, "Land Use Regulation and the Free Exercise Clause," *Columbia Law Review* 84, 6 (October 1984): 1562-89.